THE STORY OF GONDWANA

BY THE RIGHT REVEREND

EYRE CHATTERTON, D.D.

BISHOP OF NAGPUR

WITH A FOREWORD BY

The Hon. Sir Benjamin Robertson,

K.C.S.I., K.C.M.G.

GYAN

Published by

GYAN

Gyan Publishing House
5, Ansari Road
Daryaganj, New Delhi-110002
Phone: 011-47034999, 9811692060
E-mail: books@gyanbooks.com

Distribution Network
gyanbooks.com
India, USA, Canada, UK, Australia, France

ISBN : 978-81-212-9806-3 (PB)
First Published, 1916

2nd Impression 2023

Printed at: Gyan Press, Delhi.

THE STORY OF GONDWANA
Author: EYRE CHATTERTON

THE STORY OF
GONDWANA

MADAN'S PLEASURE PALACE AT GARHA

THE STORY OF GONDWANA

By The Right Reverend

EYRE CHATTERTON, D.D.

Bishop of Nagpur

WITH A FOREWORD BY

THE HON. SIR BENJAMIN ROBERTSON,

K.C.S.I., K.C.M.G.

Chief Commissioner of the Central Provinces

1916

CREST OF THE GOND KINGS

FOREWORD

It gives me much pleasure to write a few introductory words to the *Story of Gondwana* which the Bishop of Nagpur has put together from the legends and history of the past. I can remember when a boy—long before I had any thought that my lot would be cast in India—reading Forsyth's *Highlands of Central India* and being captivated by the charm of the country which he described. For the greater part of twenty-five years I have lived in the Central Provinces, the Gondwana of the Bishop's story; I have wandered over its hills and jungles, and have to the full imbibed the fascination which it exercises over all who know it, be they district officers closely in touch with the simple lives of its people, or sportsmen in pursuit of the noble game which its wide-spreading forests contain. Over none has it cast its spell more completely than the author of this little book. And to him it has, I know, been a labour of love to tell in simple language something of the old Gond kingdoms which flourished on and around the Satpuras, and briefly to trace the later history of the country which was once under their sway. May the *Story of Gondwana* help to spread more widely some knowledge of these central uplands, of their ancient past and of their manifold attractiveness at the present day.

B. ROBERTSON.

AUTHOR'S PREFACE

THE purpose of this little book is to tell briefly the Story of Gondwana, the modern Central Provinces of India. Moving up and down its plateaux and plains during the last thirteen years, seeing its old fortresses and other monuments of the past, reading isolated bits of its history in Government Gazetteers and elsewhere, I have long felt that it would be well if someone would weave together for us these scattered records into something like a connected story.

Not that Gondwana made history in the brilliant fashion which Rajasthan, and many other regions of India, did. Its earlier history is more that of one of the child races of the world. The fact, however, that it has got its own stories of romance and pathos, and that for well nigh four centuries it had its four kingdoms, ruled over by its own Gond rulers, makes all that we possess of its history worthy of being more widely known than it is at present.

A few words at the conclusion of the story on

AUTHOR'S PREFACE

Maratha rule in Gondwana, followed as it has been by our British Administration, redeem the narrative from its otherwise rather antiquarian character, and will it is hoped give our readers some idea of what their fellow-countrymen are doing in this part of India.

I have to thank Miss Alice Woodward for her charming illustrations of the Story of Lingo, and also Mr. Hands, Jubbulpore, Mr. Shalom, Nagpur, Messrs. Herzog and Higgins, Mhow, and Mr. Lawrie, Jubbulpore, for some of the illustrations in the book, which were specially taken at my request.

EYRE NAGPUR.

To My Wife

who has been my constant companion in
my journeyings in Gondwana

CONTENTS

ILLUSTRATIONS

ILLUSTRATIONS

THE STORY OF GONDWANA

CHAPTER I

OLD GONDWANA

MORE than a generation has passed since Captain Forsyth, in his well-known work on the Highlands of Central India, first sounded the praises of Gondwana. How well it deserves those praises can only be fully understood by those who, while living in the Central Provinces, retain some recollections of the deserts of Rajputana, the dusty plains of the Punjab, or the damp and low-lying country of Bengal.

The name Gondwana seems to have been given originally to a tract of country which lies to the immediate south of the Satpura Mountains, in the northern part of the modern State of Hyderabad, a region in which certain tribes of the Gond race then lived. Later on, however, it was extended to the whole of the modern Central Provinces of India.

Gondwana of old seems to have stood quite apart from the main life and civilisation of India. Its dense forests and hilly country cut it off completely from the outer world; and those who

1—(3551)

moved down from Hindustan into the Deccan, whether armies of invasion or peaceful traders, generally passed along its western side by way of the fortress of Asirgarh, and seldom penetrated into the heart of its wild jungles. And for this reason one may search in vain for anything more than a passing reference to it in general Indian history.

Certainly by far the fullest and most interesting reference to old Gondwana is to be found in the writings of Abu-l-Fazl, the Moslem chronicler of Akbar's days. Although as a highly-cultured Moslem he clearly felt contempt for the ignorant aborigines of Gondwana, still his description seems to have been fairly accurate and is decidedly amusing. It occurs when he is writing of a projected invasion of the country by Asaf Khan, the Moslem Viceroy of Manikpur.

"In the vast territories of Hindustan there is a country called Gondwana. It is the land inhabited by the tribe of Gonds, a numerous race of people, who dwell in the wilds, spend their time in eating and drinking and in the procreation of children. They are a very low race, and are held in contempt by the people of Hindustan, who look upon them as outcast from their religion and their laws. The length of the district is 300 miles. On the north lies Panna. On the south the Deccan. On the west it borders on Raisin, belonging to Malwa, and on the east Ratanpur. The country is called Garha Katanka, and contains 70,000 villages. Garha is the name

A BIT OF SATPURA SCENERY

of its chief city, and Kaṭanka is the name of a place near it. These two places have given their names to the whole country. The seat of government is the fort of Chauragarh. In former times there was no one supreme ruler, but the country was ruled by several Rajahs and Rais, and at the present time, when by the will of fortune it belongs to this race, there are several Rajahs such as Rajah Garha. The fighting men of this country are chiefly infantry, horsemen being few. From the earliest establishment of the Mohammedan power in India no monarch has been able to reduce the fortresses of this country, or annex its territory."

Now, were one asked to describe the special charm of Gondwana, a charm which distinguishes it from so much of the rest of India, one would, I think, at once point to the beautiful Satpura hills and plateaux, which lie at its very heart. Strange to say few, save those who live in Gondwana, or enterprising sportsmen in search of its big game, know of the real beauty which lies hidden away in this still rather inaccessible part of India. Even the name Satpura is hardly recognised, and the term Vindhyan, which, strictly speaking, belongs to the long range of hills and mountains which lie to the north of the Nerbudda, is still regarded by many as covering these widespread Satpura uplands which lie to the south of that river, and which reach from Khandesh to Amarkantak.

How this range received its name of Satpura is

not quite certain. Some have suggested that it is a corruption of the Indian word "Satputras," which would make it mean "seven sons," the offspring of the Vindhyans! It seems more probable, however, that it comes from the word "pura," or valley, and that it is but a name poetically descriptive of the range with its many deep valleys cutting across the main mass of mountainous country.

It is, indeed, a splendid stretch of broken highland country. Whether one finds oneself in the Gawalgarh Range near Chikalda, in the Mahadeo Range near Pachmarhi, or on the Maikal Range on the sacred plateau of Amarkantak, one is all the time in these beautiful Satpuras, far from the enervating influences of the Indian plains and enjoying an almost European climate.

What the Central Provinces would be without the Satpuras one hardly cares to think. Within its hills rise the sacred Nerbudda,[1] the most picturesque river in India, with a course of 750 miles, the Tapti with its wild and rocky bed, the Sone, the Wainganga—not to mention numerous lesser streams.

Timber of various kinds, especially teak and sal, may be seen on its hill-sides and in its valleys; and this in spite of the wanton destruction of its forests, both by axe and fire, in days gone by. Over its hills and in its valleys roam tiger,

[1] Written by old writers Narmada, "the river of soft water."

DHUPGARH, PACHMARHI

panther, bear, bison, buffalo, wild pig, deer, stag, and antelope. Nowhere in all India is there a region more beloved by the sportsman!

Nor is this region, wild though it be, without some of those sacred places of pilgrimage which are found dotted about most parts of the Indian Peninsula, and which play such a large part in the life of millions of the people of the country. Few "Tirth Sthans"[1] can compare in sacredness, so the Brahmans of the Central Provinces say, with Amarkantak, where rises the holy Nerbudda, the southern rival of Mother Ganges. Every year at certain seasons come flocking to its shrines Hindu pilgrims from all parts of India—some of whom make their pilgrimage on foot from the mouth of the river to its source, and their "darshan"[2] obtained, journey homewards on the other side of the sacred stream.

To the mysterious Cave of Mahadeo in the side of a mountain hard by Pachmarhi; to the ancient temples of Mandhata on the Nerbudda; to the temples of Ramtek, about twenty-five miles north of Nagpur; to the temples of Vishnu and the Ten Incarnations on the Wainganga, as well as to numerous smaller shrines on hill-top and by river side, thousands and thousands of the people of India journey every year, seeking "mûkti" or salvation.

Here is the land in which from early days the Gonds have lived. Not that the name Gond is

[1] Places of Pilgrimage. [2] The vision of the God.

the name which they have called themselves by; for to themselves they are, and always have been, simply Koitor, or "Men." Possibly the name Gond came to them, because in early days this part of India formed the western portion of the Old Gaur Kingdom of Bengal, and so the Dravidian Koitors, who lived in Gaur land, became known as Gonds.

Those who know Risley's work on *The People of India* will remember that the earliest and most numerous of the seven races, to which he would trace all the present people of India, is the Dravidian race. It is to this race "the ancient Britons of India," which includes Tamil, Telegu, and Canarese, and with which nearly all the conquering races of India—Aryans, Scythians, and Mongols—have so largely intermingled, that the Gond belongs.

Where these Dravidian Koitors dwelt, before they settled in the plains and uplands of the Central Provinces, is a question which cannot now be answered. The existence of a small tribe of Brahuis in Beluchistan, resembling Gonds in language and in some of their customs, have suggested to some a northern origin. The more probable view, however, is that the Gonds were an uncivilised branch of the Dravidians, who in early times moved up from the Deccan into the Central Provinces, where they made their home in company with other aboriginal races, Kols, Kurkus, and Bhils. Here they lived their

RAMTEK—THE SUMMIT OF THE HILL

primitive life in the ways they loved best, hunting always, seldom settling for long in one place, and cultivating, frequently in ways most destructive to the forests.

Then with the coming of the Aryan into India, the beginnings of a larger and more civilised life dawned for Gondwana. Hindu sages and ascetics began to appear in its wild regions, seeking for fit places for contemplation and retirement.

There is an amusing passage in the Epic of the Ramayana which shows how the highly civilised Aryans of those early days regarded the Gonds, at a time when what was known of them was principally from the mouths of those "Sadhus" or holy men. As we read it we can easily picture how these Hindu Saints were often disturbed in their devotions by the ignorant curiosity, if not worse, of the wild Gonds, who but faintly understood the meaning of the self-inflicted hardships and tortures to which these Aryan strangers from the north subjected themselves.

"The shapeless and ill-looking monsters (the Gonds) testify their abominable character by various cruel and terrific displays. These base-born wretches implicate the hermits in impure practices, and perpetrate the greatest outrages. Changing their shapes, and hiding in the thickets adjoining the hermitages, these frightful beings delight in terrifying the devotees. They cast away the sacrificial ladles and vessels, they pollute the cooked oblations, and utterly defile the offerings with blood. These faithless creatures inject frightful sounds into the ears of these faithful and austere eremites. At the time of sacrifice they snatch away the jars, the flowers, the fuel, and the sacred grass of these sober-minded men."

The "holy men" were soon followed by Rajput adventurers, who came partly as knights-errant to protect the "Rishis,"[1] and partly from the love of adventure to seek out fortunes in pastures new. Some of these Rajput knights, the younger sons of princes, married the daughters of Koitor chieftains, and quickly established themselves as rulers over parts of Gondwana. One such kingdom, the Hai-Haiya Bansi, a semi-Rajput Dynasty, had its capital at Tripuri or Tewar, about six miles from our modern Jubbulpore. Another dynasty akin to this Hai-Haiya established itself at Ratanpur, in the Bilaspur district, and remained Hindu during the Gond ascendency and on into Maratha days. Kingdoms of the semi-Rajput order arose near Seoni in the Satpuras, and south of the Satpuras, close to the modern City of Chanda. Another kingdom, whether semi-Rajput, Gaoli, or aboriginal, had its capital near to the modern town of Chhindwara.

It was these kingdoms which, without doubt, laid the beginnings of civilisation among our Gond Koitors.

Then came that strange movement in Gondwana, which makes its history almost unique in India, when, taught by their Aryan or semi-Aryan

[1] Hindu sages.

LAKE AND TEMPLES, RAMTEK

conquerors, there arose in various parts of Gondwana rulers of the same race as their Gond subjects, who, having deprived the semi-Hindu rulers of their power, began a rule which was destined to last for nearly four centuries.

Everything that we know of the rule of these Gond Rajahs points to the fact that their subjects were happy and content. Life for the most part seems to have been fairly secure both within and without. Occasional invasions from north or east, from Bundelkhand, Manikpur, or Malwa, were either repelled, or did not lead to a long occupation of Gondwana. A simple system of land settlement and land revenue was introduced in many parts, traces of which still survive in some districts of the Central Provinces.

The value of water storage was fully realised by these old Gond rulers. In 1865, after visiting the northern part of the Chanda district through which the Wainganga flows, and referring to a number of tanks which had been made by the old Gond Rajahs of Chanda in that district, Sir R. Temple says

" The number and size of these tanks is certainly remarkable. In some parts they cluster thick round the feet of the hills. From the summit of one hill, no less than thirty-seven tanks were visible. They are, as the people themselves told me, the very life of the place, and the object to which much of the industry and capital of the people are devoted. The two staple foods of the district, rice and sugar-cane, are entirely dependent on the water-supply from these tanks. Not only have these large sheets of water been formed by damming up streams with heavy earthwork dykes, but masonry escapes and sluices, and channels, have also been constructed. Some of the sluices, as headworks for irrigation channels, present an elaborate apparatus, creditable to the skill and ingenuity of the people."

Well-built fortresses like Deogarh, Chauragarh, and Kherla, splendidly situated on hill-tops, as well as other buildings all more or less of a modified Saracenic or Islamic pattern, arose in various parts of the country. In fact so much of civilisation was introduced into Gondwana by these Gond rulers, that some have thought, and still think, that we are mistaken in regarding them as Gonds pure and simple. Undoubtedly there were cases when Gond princes married Rajput wives (as was the case with the famous queen Durgavati), but it does not seem that we have solid ground for believing that this was other than exceptional. For the most part we may think of the Rajahs of these four dynasties as Gonds pure and simple, who had raised themselves by superior ability and force of character to the position of rulers over their people. Nor need we regard this as making too great a claim for the capacity of an aboriginal race, when we see what education has done, and is doing, for a kindred race, the aborigines of Chhota Nagpur, and when we meet some of the present Gond rulers of our Feudatory States in the Central Provinces.

And so it came about that nearly 600 years ago, four independent Gond kingdoms arose, more or less simultaneously, in Gondwana; the northern with its chief city at Garha, only three miles from Jubbulpore; the two central with their capitals at Deogarh, in the Chhindwara district, and at Kherla in the Betul district; and the southern with its capital, first at Sirpur, and then at Chanda. And these kingdoms lasted on for nearly four centuries until the Maratha for a time introduced chaos into this primitive cosmos. Then for nearly 100 years the Maratha held a by no means beneficial sway over this fair land, until a brighter day dawned for Gondwana, when law and order of a type far higher than had been seen before was introduced by the coming of British rule.

The story of these four Gond kingdoms is the theme of the early portion of our narrative. That a full history of the Gond Dynasties can ever be written is vain to expect, as the materials for such a history simply do not exist. We must remember that reading and writing were unknown to the Gonds, save what was introduced amongst them by the Hindus. No Gond literature was ever produced. That some sort of culture, however, existed in and around the Gond courts of Mandla, Garha, Kherla, Deogarh, and Chanda, is fairly certain. Brahmans were generally to be found in attendance on the old Gond Rajahs whose services were used for the casting of horoscopes, for purposes of worship and sacrifice, and for many domestic, social, and ceremonial functions. Moslem influence, too, came into the courts of these Rajahs as history records, and as the ruined buildings at Chauragarh, Deogarh, Chanda and elsewhere clearly indicate.

And though the Gondwana of the days of the Four Kingdoms has passed away, and wild regions, in which formerly the roar of the tiger, the chatter of the monkey, and other such denizens of the jungle, alone disturbed its deep and long silences, resound to-day with the shrill shriek of the locomotive and the horn of the motor, still the broad-faced Gond lives on in his old surroundings in number about 2,000,000. Nor, too, amidst all the highly organised machinery of British rule, or the growing evidences of our western civilisation, in coal and manganese mining, as well as in other forms of industrial life, have all traces of Gond rule quite faded away. For Gond Rajahs may still be seen who rule their small Feudatory States on the borders of British administered districts; and petty Gond chieftains still live on in their villages and "Jagirs" as did their ancestors, riding on their elephants, and accompanied by their miniature escorts.

CHAPTER II

GARHA AND THE NORTHERN GOND KINGDOM

> The Kingdom of the Gonds is gone,
> But noble memories remain,
> And with a loving awe we scan
> The battle page, which ends thy reign.
>
> —DURGAVATI, *Pekin.*

FEW stations in the plains of India can compare with Jubbulpore for the charm of its surroundings. Lying close to the northern edge of the Satpuras, and in the valley of the Nerbudda, not far from where that picturesque river leaves the wilder regions of Mandla, and enters a broad stretch of fertile country which lies between the Vindhyan and Satpura ranges, it is certainly set in a most attractive stretch of country.

What however most impresses one, at first sight, in its immediate neighbourhood, are certain of its hills covered as they are by huge fantastically-shaped boulders. There they lie like the moraine of a great glacier, which may have covered this valley in bygone ages, when this part of India was held fast in the grip of the ice age. Nowhere are these great boulders scattered more widely, and in greater disorder, than in one long low range of hills lying to the west of Jubbulpore, beneath which at one time lay the capital of Northern Gondwana.

THE STORY OF GONDWANA

Few of those who, on their way to the famous Marble Rocks, pass through the long straggling village of Garha, realise that this was a royal city for nearly 500 years, and that the quaint building, the Madan Mahal, which stands out like a watch-tower on the summit of the hill, poised on two gigantic rocks, was part of the pleasure palace which the Gond Rajah Madan Singh reared for himself, and from which he used, doubtless, to gaze down complacently on his pretty capital and the rich valley which lay beyond it.

Yet there are not wanting even to-day silent witnesses to the times when kings lived and ruled in Garha. Tanks built by many a Rajah, and especially by the famous Gond Queen Durgavati; temples, now fast decaying, built to commemorate victories, or to propitiate gods and goddesses; vast plantations of mango trees planted by one famous Gond Rajah, all recall the bygone days of the greatness of Garha.

With the Buddhist, or Hindu dynasties, which ruled in this part of India, centuries before the Gonds rose to power, we are not here concerned. Doubtless it was by them that the first elements of Aryan civilisation were introduced amongst the aboriginal Gonds. One semi-Rajput dynasty, the Kalachuri kings of the Hai-Hai Bansi line, certainly reigned in these regions for more than two centuries, before the Gonds came into power. Their capital, however, was not at Garha but at Tewar or Tripuri, three or four miles beyond it

OLD GOND PALACE AT GARHA

on the road to the Marble Rocks. Then at length, after centuries of foreign rule, probably about the thirteenth century of our era, the subject race produced a man of its own fit to rule over it, and the Hindu ruler had to give place to the Gond.

Jadurai was the Gond hero who first came to the front. Coming as a young man from his home in the region of the river Godaveri, he entered the service of the Kalachuri Rajah. There he learnt his first lessons in state-craft, and there also he learnt the weak points in his master's character and rule. Having learnt these lessons he departed, but only for a season. A successful marriage with the daughter of the Gond Chieftain Nagdeo, of the fortress town of Mandla, sixty miles further up the Nerbudda river, was the next step in his career, which gave him the status which his lowly birth as the son of a village patel had hitherto denied him. His position was now assured amongst the Gonds. Associating with himself a clever adventurer, one Surbhi Pathak, who had once, like himself, been in the service of the Kalachuri Rajah, he carefully laid his plans, and eventually succeeded in overturning the rule of the Kalachuris and usurping their power. From this time the Gond rule began in northern Gondwana, a rule which was destined to last for fully four centuries.

There is, however, another version of the story, as told in Sir W. Sleeman's history of Garha Mandla, which differs considerably from the above.

According to it Jadurai was a Hindu who took service with a certain Hindu Rajah, and accompanied his master on pilgrimage to Amarkantak, the source of the Nerbudda. One night while guarding the Royal Tent he chanced to see two Gond men and a woman followed by a large monkey. As they passed him, the monkey gazed into his face, and dropped some peacock's feathers, and at the conclusion of his watch retired to rest. In his sleep the goddess Nerbudda appeared to him in a dream, and told him that the people he had seen were not mortals, but were no less than Rama, Sita, and Laxman, the monkey being the God Hanuman. The feathers were a sign that he would one day attain to sovereign power. He was, however, to visit as soon as possible a Brahman recluse at Ramnagar, named Surbhi Pathak, who would be his "Guru."[1] Jadurai immediately gave up his post with the Rajah and proceeded to Ramnagar. There he found Surbhi Pathak, who to his amazement informed him that the goddess Nerbudda had also appeared to him, and told him of Jadurai's great destiny. He then led Jadurai into the midstream of the Nerbudda, and made him take a solemn oath, that if ever he should become king he would appoint him as his first minister. The oath taken, he advised Jadurai to proceed to Garha and offer his services to the Gond Rajah. At this time, the Rajah had an only child, a daughter named

[1] Religious teacher.

Ratana Vali, and finding himself in declining health, and without hope of a son, he took counsel of his leading advisers as to the choice of a son-in-law. They bade him leave the choice to God, and as a means of ascertaining the Divine will, advised him to assemble a great multitude of his subjects on the river bank, and then let loose a blue jay amongst them. If the bird alighted on the head of any one, he was clearly marked out to be the one chosen of God to succeed him. The Prince was delighted with this simple solution of his difficulties, and on the day appointed released a jay in the midst of an immense concourse of his people. It flew straight to Jadurai, and alighted upon his head. At first, Jadurai, being a Hindu, felt some scruples about allying himself with a Gond maiden, but the difficulty was soon got over by his astute spiritual guide, who stipulated that Jadurai should never eat from the hand of his bride, though their issue, if any, should be heirs to the throne.

Of Jadurai's immediate successors we know nothing save their names, which are duly recorded in a genealogy prepared by order of the Gond king Hirde Shah, and now found on a Sanskrit tablet on the walls of the Gond palace at Ramnagar, near Mandla.

It is to Sangram Shah that northern Gondwana owes its real greatness and fame. Until he came to the "Gadi," [1] about A.D. 1480, the sway of the

[1] Throne.

Gond kings was confined entirely to the country around Jubbulpore and Mandla. A man of large ambitions and high courage, he was not content with his small kingdom, and during his reign annexed large portions of the Nerbudda Valley and the districts now called Saugor and Damoh, as well as much of the modern state of Bhopal. At his death the original four districts which formed this kingdom had become no less than fifty-four. Desiring to defend his new possessions in the Nerbudda Valley, he built the stronghold of Chauragarh about ninety miles west of Jubbulpore, from which he could keep guard over a large part of the valley, and to which he and his descendants could always retreat when their country was invaded. Later on we shall have occasion to speak more fully of this splendid fortress.

Nor did he forget to add to the beauties of his capital at Garha, for to the present day one of its most picturesque little lakes bears his name, and one of its finest temples, dedicated to the fierce god Bhairava, was built by him.

Sangram Shah was undoubtedly the most distinguished prince of the northern kingdom. Thoughtful for the future of his kingdom, and proud of his son Dalpat's daring and splendid appearance, Sangram Shah decided that he must find for him a worthy partner. His choice fell on Durgavati, the daughter of the Chandela Raja of Mahoba, a woman of great beauty and, as events proved, of even greater character. But for a

LAKE AT GARHA

time the fates seemed adverse to the marriage. Though it was clear that Durgavati was ready and desirous to wed with this splendid Gond youth, another suitor of Rajput blood also sought her hand, and objections to the marriage on the ground of caste were raised by the Rajah of Mahoba. Only one way was open to Dalpat, so Durgavati privately informed him. He must win her by his sword, or else for ever cease to think of her. And Dalpat Shah joyously accepted the challenge, and with his army of Gonds marched northwards to do battle with a hostile prospective father-in-law and a hated rival. Fortune smiled on his efforts, and at the end of the battle victory was his. It was a romantic wooing, but the union which followed was destined to last only for four short years. Then Dalpat, still young in years, though great in valour, was gathered to his fathers, and Durgavati was left with her three-year old son, Bir Narayan, to guard the great inheritance which Sangram had bequeathed to Dalpat. It is to the way in which she fulfilled this trust that she owes her unique name, and fame, in the annals of Gondwana.

From time to time in the history of India women have appeared, around whose lives a halo of romance must for ever linger. Who that has read the stoιy of the Ramayan can ever forget Sita, the heroine of that great epic, the faithful wife, who wore the " white flower of a blameless life" ? And Sita has had many spiritual daughters in succeeding ages whose faithfulness, courage, purity, and devotion, have added fresh laurels to Indian womanhood. No one who has visited the famous fortress of Chitor in Rajputana, and read of its prolonged and deadly struggles with Delhi, will forget the story of the beautiful Padmani, who preferred death to the harem of Akbar, and led a great company of the ladies of her court into the flames, while the flower of Rajput chivalry was dying under its walls, overpowered by the hosts of the Moghul. Nor can anyone who has visited Mandu, most fascinating of India's ruined cities, on the slopes of the Vindhyans, read the somewhat similar story of Queen Rupmati's devotion and death without some thrill of sympathy. It is in this noble company of Indian heroines that Dalpat Shah's young widow Durgavati is worthy to be placed.

For fifteen years after Dalpat's death, Durgavati reigned over the widespread territories of Sangram wisely and well. Strong fortresses which still stand, though in decay, such as Chauragarh in the Narsinghpur district, Singorgarh in the Damoh district, thirty miles north of Jubbulpore (for a time Dalpat's capital), and fortresses in Bhopal, such as Chaukigarh and Gunergarh, all remind one of the strength and extent of her kingdom.

Her son Bir Narayan was approaching manhood, when a terrible blow fell on the northern Gond kingdom, which was to end her happy rule.

For some time Asaf Khan, the Moghul Viceroy at Manikpur, to the north of Damoh, had been gazing with covetous eyes on the great fertile valley of the Nerbudda, then administered by Durgavati. The prize seemed easy to win. The reports of her great beauty and wealth had made its acquisition doubly desirable.

Asaf Khan's mind was soon made up. At the head of an army he marched southwards on Garha. The news of his advance aroused no fear in the mind of this Rajput Boadicea. At the head of her troops, mounted on her royal elephant, she moved forth to meet him from Singorgarh, the most northern fortress of her dominions.

But the Gonds, though brave, were no match for Asaf Khan's trained soldiers, and Durgavati was compelled to retreat. Hard pressed by the army of Asaf Khan, the battle was resumed somewhere between Garha and Mandla. Again Moghul arms proved too strong, and Durgavati, who had herself been wounded, was preparing to fly, when it was discovered that the river (most probably the Hinghan, one of the tributaries of the Nerbudda) on the line of her flight, was in flood, and escape was impossible. Then true to the traditions of her race, she preferred death to dishonour, and died by her own hand, rather than fall into the hands of Akbar's Viceroy.

So perished this noble woman, whose name should always be cherished as amongst the noblest of India's daughters. One fine stretch of water between Jubbulpore and Garha still bears her name, the Rani Tal ; and her simple tomb, called appropriately by the villagers the "Chabutra," about ten miles from Jubbulpore, is still held in reverence by all who live in its neighbourhood and by strangers who pass it by.

TOMB OF QUEEN DURGAVATI

CHAPTER III

CHAURAGARH AND THE NORTHERN GOND KINGDOM

THE death of Durgavati was a deep calamity to her devoted people. Bir Narayan was still but a youth, who had as yet hardly faced any of the responsibilities of life. From the battle-field near Jubbulpore he was hurried by his advisers to the fortress of Chauragarh, which his grandfather Sangram Shah had built on the northern crest of the Satpuras.

No one who visits Chauragarh to-day can fail to be impressed with the enormous natural strength of the fortress, embracing as it does within its circle of defences two long and lofty hills which approach one another at an angle of 45°, and which are connected by a slight depression. It was clearly a fortress capable of holding a large garrison, and must in olden days have been almost impregnable. Thither in hot pursuit of the young Gond prince came Asaf Khan and his army. Asaf Khan was more than a match for his youthful adversary. By treachery or daring, or by a combination of both, Chauragarh soon passed into his hands. Bir Narayan fell in the sack of the fortress, and the ladies of the court, in wild fear lest they should suffer dishonour, set fire to the palace. Only two of them survived—

Bir Narayan's betrothed wife, and Queen Durgavati's sister. For them an unkind fate decreed places in Akbar's harem at Delhi. If indeed the record of the loot which fell into Asaf Khan's hands is to be trusted, the wealth of the northern Gond kings must at this time have been considerable:— "101 cooking pots full of large and valuable gold coins besides jewels, gold and silver plate and images of the gods," these were but portions of the spoil. Greatest of all were the number of elephants which Asaf Khan took, and which numbered fully 1,000.

The story, however, goes on to say that Asaf Khan took good care that none of the jewels got further than Manikpur, and that his royal master, as the result of the conquest of northern Gondwana, only received 300 indifferent elephants!

For some years after these tragic events Asaf Khan appears to have held Garha as an independent principality, probably with the intention of remaining there. Warnings, however, from Delhi made him realise the wisdom of renouncing any idea of breaking away from his allegiance to the Emperor, and so in due course he returned to Manikpur. Asaf Khan's invasion clearly marks an epoch in the history of North Gondwana.

Writing in 1825, Sir W. Sleeman tells us that "from this time onwards local tradition speaks of regular intercourse between this Gond kingdom and Delhi." For the future the Moghuls exercised something like suzerainty over North Gondwana.

CHAURAGARH FORT, TANK ON SUMMIT

It is interesting to note that the oldest rupees which have been unearthed in this region belong to the reign of Akbar.

On Asaf Khan's withdrawal, Chandar Shah, an uncle of the ill-fated Bir Narayan and younger brother of Dalpat Shah, was proclaimed Raja of Garha-Mandla, and was recognised as such by the Emperor Akbar. In view of this recognition, Chandar Shah was persuaded by the astute Akbar to part with that portion of his territory which now forms the kingdom of Bhopal. Chandar Shah's successor, Madhukar Shah, came to the throne of his fathers with the fatal stain of his elder brother's blood on his hands. That he felt his crime deeply is evidenced by the fact that some years later his remorse drove him to take his own life by voluntarily incarcerating himself in a dry hollow pipal tree (one of the sacred trees of India), and then being burnt to death.

Of Madhukar Shah the fact is recorded that he was the first of his line to visit the Moghul Court for the purpose of doing homage to the Emperor. After this it seems to have been customary for the eldest son and heir of Northern Gondwana to spend some time at Delhi, where doubtless he was initiated into the manners and customs of courts and the mysteries of diplomacy and state-craft.

The news of Madhukar Shah's self-immolation came to the ear of his eldest son Prem Narayan while with the Emperor at Delhi. Leaving his eldest son Hirde Shah to represent him at the

Imperial Court, the Gond Raja hastened back to Garha. Little could he have realised that a trivial act of discourtesy on his part, in failing to return the ceremonial visit of Bir Singh Deo, Rajah of Orchha, was to bring on his country the horrors of a second invasion. As the story runs, this proud prince of Orchha was so angered at this discourtesy of the young Gond Rajah, that on his death-bed he made his son, Jhujhar Singh, swear to avenge this insult by the invasion and conquest of Garha. It is possible, however, that an additional reason may have made it easier for Jhujhar Singh to induce his followers to carry out his father's unreasonable behest. The Gonds, as aborigines, had no respect for the sacred cow, which they used for ploughing, and whose flesh was always welcome at their feasts. As such treatment of the sacred animal would, to the Hindu Rajputs, be "Anathema," Jhujhar Singh would have experienced no difficulty in persuading his subjects that such a war was a "holy" one. And so from a failure to observe the etiquette of kings, as well as from an ignorant adherence to the customs of their ancestors, the kingdom of Garha-Mandla had to endure its second invasion.

Again, as in the time of Asaf Khan, Chauragarh was the chief point of attack. On this occasion, however, the Rajput failed where the Moslem had succeeded. For several months the army of Jhujhar Singh closely invested the fortress, but without making any impression upon it. Then,

CHAURAGARH FORT, WATCH TOWER

where might had failed, treachery was called in. Jhujhar Singh feigned weariness of his unsuccessful enterprise, and withdrew his army to some distance from Chauragarh. A message was sent by him to Prem Narayan indicating his readiness to retire from Gondwana, and asking for an interview. Suspecting nothing, Prem Narayan descended with his Gond escort from his fortress, only to discover, when too late, that he was the victim of foul treachery. The common story is that the vindictive Jhujhar Singh immediately ordered his enemy's head to be removed; but the story which Gond tradition loves to remember is a different one. It pictures Prem Narayan surrounded by overpowering numbers, and in his despair dedicating his head to his patron goddess. It further pictures the goddess placing her magic sword in the hands of the headless warrior, and his foes in dismay flying before him. Even now the Gonds believe that the head of Prem Narayan, turned to stone, is within the fortress, while his petrified body lies at the foot of the hill. With Prem Narayan's death the fortress soon succumbed, and with it for a brief period North Gondwana came into the hands of the marauding Bundelas.

But Jhujhar's triumph was short-lived. Messengers soon came to Delhi to tell Hirde Shah of the treachery of Jhujhar, and of his father's tragic death. Post-haste he came to his people, only stopping for a short time in Bhopal to secure the aid of its chieftain against a common foe. Then when his preparations were complete he fearlessly gave battle to his father's and his country's foe, and with complete success. Jhujhar was killed and his army was routed.

Only once again did these Bundelas venture on an extensive raid into the Nerbudda Valley. As they turned their faces northwards and laughed at their success in "singeing the beard of these savage Gonds," their mirth was suddenly turned into blind unreasoning fear. Their wagons, laden with loot, had crossed the sacred Nerbudda, and were struggling up its northern banks, when an invisible and mysterious power drew them all back into the river. No effort of theirs could stay them as they rolled backward, and as in some mysterious way the conviction that the hostile spirit of the headless Prem Narayan was present came over them, the Bundela warriors terror-stricken, fled northwards never to return.

To Hirde Shah North Gondwana owes much. It was his aim to strengthen and consolidate the possessions of his ancestors, which had already shrunk somewhat by concessions to certain of his neighbours. To him is ascribed the planting of 100,000 mango trees in the neighbourhood of Garha, and the construction of the fine reservoir, the Ganga Sagar, near Garha. To him also we owe the large Gond palace at Ramnagar, twelve miles from Mandla. Certainly few buildings in India enjoy a more beautiful situation than does

PALACE AT RAMNAGAR

this palace, situated as it is high above the banks of the Nerbudda, and overlooking a fine stretch of river. One can readily understand with what feelings of security and peace Hirde Shah must have spent his days when residing at Ramnagar in the fastnesses of Mandla, and away from the open country of Garha.

CHAPTER IV

HIRDE SHAH AND THE PEDIGREE OF THE GOND KINGS

THE Gond king, Hirde Shah, was clearly a man of this world. His days in Delhi, where at the Emperor's Court he mixed with many of the leading princes of India, had made him feel the force of pride of race. Under his orders a pedigree of the Royal House of Gondwana was prepared and inscribed in an enduring form on the walls of his palace at Ramnagar, near Mandla. This truly wonderful work was entrusted to a learned Hindu, by name Jaya Govinda. Few of those unacquainted with Oriental processes of imagination have, I venture to think, ever read anything quite like this pedigree. For this reason I have thought it well to let my readers see most of this family tree. It may be well to point out that the earlier portion of this pedigree is pure fiction. The clerk, Jaya Govinda, was under orders to produce a good long pedigree. He carried out his task most thoroughly. Jadurai, called in the pedigree Yadavaraya, who was in reality quite a modern person, was projected by this clever pedigree-maker into the dim past, where gods and heroes are indistinguishable. Among his descendants celebrated Hindu heroes like Ramchandra, Krishna, and Prithwi Raj, are introduced without any regard to history. Only when we meet with Madan Singh in this illustrious company do we touch on solid ground at all, and to him, as we have already seen, we owe the Madan Mahal at Garha. But the full eloquence of the pedigree is reserved for Sangram, Dalpat, Durgavati, Madhukar Shah, Prem Narayan, and Hirde Shah himself.

THE PEDIGREE[1]

Glory to the auspicious Ganesa.[2] The auspicious Trivikrama,[3] the beautiful, bears sway.

1. Salutation to thee, Vishnu, who, though as if in thy entirety, manifoldly manifested, art yet assuredly unapprehended in any of thy real nature whatsoever.

2. In the country of Gadha was a monarch, Yadavaraya, a sea of virtuous qualities. His son was Madhavasinha; from whom sprang Jagannatha.

3–13. Then occur the names of no less than forty of Hirde Shah's ancestors in succession, among whom occur the three well-known incarnations of the god Vishnu, Narsingh,[4] Ramchandra, and Krishna, besides others famous in Hindu

[1] Translated by Fitz-Edward Hall, D.C.L., presented to the American Oriental Society, 17th Oct., 1860, and published in the Society's *Journal*, Vol. VII, p. 13 *et seq.* (1862).

[2] The elephant-headed god, the god of Prosperity.

[3] Trivi Krama. An epithet of Vishnu in his Baman Incarnation. (The one who took three steps.)

[4] Narsingh, the Man-Lion Incarnation of Vishnu.

Mythology like Rudra[1], Jagannath,[2] Vasudeva.[3] Madan Singh, the builder of the Madan Mahal, is also mentioned. Sangram is spoken of as the son of Arjun, the famous warrior.

14. His son was Sangramasahi; an exterminating fire to his foes, as if they had been masses of cotton-wool; the radiance of whose grandeur being spread abroad, the midday sun became like a mere spark.

15. By which king, when he had reduced the orb of the earth, two and fifty fastnesses were constructed; indestructible from their excellent fortifications, which were like adamant, and possessed the firm strength of mountains, because of their water.

16. Of him gem of princes, King Dalapati was the son; of unsullied glory, to hymn forth whose fame the Lord of serpents[4] hoped that all his mouths would enduringly remain.

17. To the dust of whose feet—since his hand was constantly moist with the water of bounty, and as he was diligent in the remembrance of Hari,[5] a refuge to those who were brought under his authority—to him even people infected with the quality of passion continually had recourse.

18. His consort was Durgavati; in sooth the increase of fortune to suppliants; accumulated holiness actually personified the very bound of earth's prosperity.

19. This Purandara[6] of the circuit of the earth

[1] Rudra, a Vedic god, identified with Agni.

[2] Jagannath, an appearance of Vishnu.

[3] Vasudeva, the father of Krishna.

[4] Either an epithet of Vishnu with the cobra hood over him, or Sesha.

[5] A name of the god Vishnu.

[6] A name for the beneficent Rain god, "Indra."

having demised, Durgavati consecrated on the seat of royalty their son, of three years age, the illustrious Viranarayana, so called.

20. By whom Durgavati of repute blazoned throughout the triple universe, the whole earth was rendered as it were another by interminable glittering Hemachalas,[1] in its stately golden edifices in number untold, in its abundance of valuable jewels everywhere tossing about, by innumerable Indra's elephants, in its herds of spirited elephants.

21. Who, Durgavati, with her daily occupation, which consisted in unceasing donations of millions of horses, elephants, and pieces of gold, depreciated in semblance by her exalted celebrity, the universal honour of Kamadhenu.[2]

22. Mounted on an elephant in person, and by force over-mastering in many a battle prepotent adversaries, ever studious for the safeguard of her subjects, she superseded, to all appearance, the protectors of the regions.

23. Appropriating no less than the tribute of kings their illustrious world-diffused splendour, he, the fortunate Viranarayana as was his appellation, of renown illimitable, entered on adolescence.

24. Subsequently, some time having elapsed, Asaf Khan with an army was deputed by King Akbar, Puruhuta[3] of the earth, all but compeer of Partha,[4] for the purpose of levying a contribution.

[1] A mythical golden mountain, Mount Meru, north of the Himalayas.

[2] A fabled cow capable of producing an inexhaustible supply of all objects of desire.

[3] Puruhuta = the god Indra.

[4] Arjuna, one of the five Pandu Princes.

25. At the close of an engagement by this great warrior, a Bhima[1] in prowess, whose armaments depressed the face of the earth, Durgavati, though she had vanquished his entire army,

26. Being vexed with countless hostile arrows, clove her own head, in an instant, with a sword in her hand, as she sat on her elephant; whereupon she penetrated the solar sphere, as did her son.

27. Then was inaugurated the younger brother of King Dalpati, Chandrasahi; an asylum to the lordless people, a treasury, so to speak, of magnificence; the inextinguishable irradiator of his whole race; opulent in glory.

28. Of the wives of whose antagonists the trees, with their thorns, snatched away the robes and laid hold of the tresses; while they, the ladies, exhibiting conflagrations in the sheen of their persons suddenly exposed consumed them, the trees, with their sighs; and ever, from very wretchedness, they bore the bark of shrubs for clothing. Thus, in the forests, did they, in a manner wage strife with things immovable.

29. Of this monarch a son was born, King Madukarasahi, as of Siva, Shanmukha,[2] of honourable note; as if a receptacle of noble greatness.

30. By the triumphs of whom—resistless in enterprise, as repelling and destroying the impetuous and overweening, stricken deaf with the rushing torrent of the clamour of his drums, enough to drown the roar of huge compact cataclysmal rain-clouds newly come—achieved by the

[1] Bhima, another of the five Pandu Princes; a great warrior.

[2] Shanmukha, a son of Shiva, generally called Kartikeya—one with six mouths.

might of his arm, and applauded by multitudes of his lieges, the quarters responsive oftentimes to this very day manifestly cause shame to their eight presiding deities.

31. The son of this king was the fortunate Premanarayana; accomplishing, through his affluence, the desires of the pure; the collective lustre of the tribe of warriors; the incorporate energy of Smara;[1] a domicile of good report; the exaltation of his family; the complete estate of virtue; the measure of creative cunning; a repository of merits; no path for reproach.

32. Of whom—humbling and routing a whole troop of chieftains, by the fresh dense surge of thousands of legions terrible with serried phalanxes of most infuriate elephants redolent from the Vindhyas—the adversaries, whose slumbers were straightway broken when first they perceived his refulgent grandeur, do not even yet readily leave the caves of the mountains, though separated from their wives.

33. Kings indeed presumptuous should be rigorously coerced on the battlefield; but one ought not to harbour animosity. Fame should be enhanced by performing meritorious acts unremittingly among the people; but one must not foster pride. Their wishes should at all times whatever promptly be granted to petitioners; but one must not wait to be entreated. Such, obviously, is the duty of the rulers of this world; and for the justness of these maxims the practice of Premasahi is an argument.

34. Of him the auspicious lord Premasahi was born another, the illustrious lord Hridaya, as he was called, a source of happiness to the pious, and

[1] Smara or Kamadeva, the Indian Cupid, slain by Shiva.

mighty like his forefathers: as arises the year; teeming with lunar days of numerous moments; whose appearance commences with the first day of the moon's increase; ever augmented by months growing with nycthemera; alternating with light and dark fortnights.[1]

35. Thoroughly defending the entire world, this monarch especially befriends the helpless; as a cloud rains equably as it may, yet irrigates most copiously the low places with its water.

36. By which king have been assigned to Brahmans, with the prescribed formalities of grants on plates of copper, sundry villages; begirt by lines of elegant gardens, rising with stuccoed dwelling-houses, inhabited by a substantial tenantry, provided with pellucid meres stocked with water-lilies, adorned with ample and frequent habitations of herdsmen, and with spacious tillage round about.

37. Which king keeps up all his vast domain: where, from goodly mansions, may be recognised diversities of construction: which is visible from its fine towns and palm-trees; delightful from attachment to the body of revealed and memorial law; independent of its borderlands; captivating the heart by the presence of proper roads; and easy of attainment only by men challenging admiration; and he is likewise conversant in the science of melody and the dance, with its refinements.

38. The whole earth and all potentates are enclosed in the hand of lord Hridaya. By the same were traced, midway on a golden wall, as it had been fifty immense elephants.

[1] The Hindus divide the month into two periods, the moonlit and the dark.

TEMPLE OF SIDDHNATH, MANDHATA

39. It has been no matter of surprise at all, that a minute stationary butt was transfixed by him, who, with his shafts, can sever, almost simultaneously, at quite distinct points, an arrow launched obliquely.

40. Who, at the time of the chase, hunting on foot, has, all of a sudden, slain, with his bolt, a tiger assaulting from aloft, of forefront fearful as an enormous serpent's and formidable. Regarding whom is this speech of Indra, when he was thus bespoken.

41. "Prithee tell us, Vishnu, why art thou dejected?" "What! is it not known to you, worthy deities, that this king Hridaya makes, on the earth, of Brahmans, many Satakratus?"[1]

42. Of this lord of the earth the queen is Sundari Devi, the abode of prosperity, as being, in effect, the wealth of merit, embodied.

43. From whom are constantly obtained, by Brahmans, elephants, beauteous as dusky clouds, with the copious ichor of their frontal exudations; given with the water of donation ever at hand; precluding to the needy the cause of clustering miseries.

44. Who shines resplendent throughout the world with her fair fame earned unceasingly by endowments in succession as ordained; which endowments, finding, among the nations, straitened scope for encomium, reached to heaven; giving forth such effulgence as a hundred autumnal moons would realise.

45. Who observes, without intermission, the holy ordinances, by innumerable conservatory liberalities, in the making of reservoirs, gardens, ponds, and the like, entailing munificent gratuities.

[1] One who offers a hundred sacrifices = Indra.

46. Who, establishing this fane, has enshrined therein Vishnu, Sambhu,[1] Ganesa, Durga,[2] and Tarani.[3]

47. Who is there capable of fitly eulogising her, by whom an abode has been provided to the adorable Sankara,[4] Sridhara,[5] and others, deities as they are?

48. Who, the queen, evermore pays worship to the gods and to the comely Trivikrama as chief, in the Brahmans whom she employs in it, and by dispensing good cheer, by keeping jubilees, and by bestowing unmeted riches. Moreover, by the command of the king, the youthful Mrigavati constantly brings various articles of food for oblation to Muradwit.[6]

49. Surpassingly victorious is the lord king Hridaya and pre-eminent in power by his clemency; even as the moon, with its beams, subdues by the force of gentleness.

50. At his behest, the clerkly Jayagovinda—son of the learned Mandana, of favourable repute, versed in the exegesis of the Mimansa,[7] a master of dialectic, and proficient in expounding the sacred oracles and their supplements—has composed, in epitome, this account relating to the sovereigns of his lineage.

51. By dexterous artificers, named Sinhasahi,

[1] Sambhu = Shiva.

[2] Durga = an Incarnation of the goddess Parvati, wife of Shiva.

[3] Tarani = The Sun.

[4] Sankara = Shiva.

[5] Sridhara = Vishnu.

[6] Krishna, who slew the demon Mura.

[7] One of the six schools of Hindu philosophy

Dayarama, and Bhagirtha, this temple was constructed.

52. On the day of Vishnu, the light fortnight of Jyeshtha, in the year one thousand seven hundred and twenty-four, this record was transcribed by Sadasiva, and engraven by these skilful artisans aforesaid.

Friday, the 12th day of the bright semilunation of Jyeshtha, in the year of Samvat 1724.

From Hirde Shah onwards the history of Northern Gondwana moved away from Chauragarh and Garha, and centred more and more around Mandla. Its interest also rapidly declined. No great man or woman appeared in its pages. Pretty intrigue was constantly manifest. It was a house divided against itself, and it could not stand. No one arose to arrest its decay. District after district fell away from it. Its revenues were spent in buying off its enemies, and when at length the Peshwa appeared, there was no power left to resist his insolent demands.

And so, when Narhar Shah, the last of its ruling princes, was defeated by the Marathas near Garha, and sent to spend the rest of his days as a prisoner in the fortress of Khurai in Saugor, one almost breathes a sigh of relief, mingled it may be with regret, at the inglorious termination of the once famous Garha-Mandla dynasty.

Just for a moment the descendants of these Gond Rajahs appeared again in the pages of history. Pensioners of the British Raj, father and son were convicted during the mutiny of 1857 of a plot to foully murder the English residents of Jubbulpore, an unworthy return to the power which had saved them from the Marathas. "Blown from the guns!" Can anyone imagine a more wretched fate for the descendants of Sangram and Dalpat Shah? And now a family, which claims its descent from Queen Durgavati, lives in an obscure village of Damoh, fed by the bounty of the Ruling Power.

DEOGARH, FORTRESS

CHAPTER V

DEOGARH, AND THE EASTERN MIDDLE GOND KINGDOM

FAR away from Northern Garha, where the southern slopes of the Satpuras approach the plain country to the north of the Deccan, stands the fortress of Deogarh. Beneath it in former days lay the city, but to-day almost nothing remains but the tombs of the Gond kings.

Those whose love of the past leads them across the fifteen miles of jungle country which now separates Deogarh from the main road leading from Nagpur to Chhindwara, will never regret it, for the sight of the Gond fortress of Deogarh crowning a lofty hill and surrounded on three sides by deep valleys is an unexpected and striking one. Surely never was a spot more wisely selected for an old-world fortress than this, where secure from attack, and hidden away from the outer world, its rulers could dominate the rich lands which lay to the south, watered by the Wainganga and Kanhan, and levy toll on those adventurous merchants who dared to move across the wild country which separated the Deccan from Hindustan.

Here it was that for long years the Gond kings of the Eastern Middle Kingdom held sway. Before their day men of another race had ruled over the wild Gond race in these regions.

Whether those rulers were Rajputs of the Aryan stock, or, as is more probable, Gaolis or shepherd kings, Scytho-Dravidians by race, though Hindus by religion, is a matter which does not deeply concern us. Suffice it to say that, as in other parts of Gondwana so here, the Gonds only came into power and produced their rulers after some centuries of Hindu ascendency. Probably the period of Gond ascendency at Deogarh was somewhat later than in the Northern Kingdom.

Jatba[1] was the first of his race to rule over his own people, and his rule did not commence till the fifteenth century. Many are the stories told of his greatness. To the Gonds his birth itself was miraculous. Born of a Gond virgin under a bean plant, he was appropriately named Jatba (the bean). A large cobra protected the infant from the scorching rays of the sun, as his village mother worked in the fields. When he grew up he took service in the Court of the twin Gaoli Rajahs Ransur and Ghansur. His strength was enormous. His arms were of exceptional length and power, which made him an antagonist whom few cared to face. On one occasion when asked to kill some buffaloes for a sacrifice at the feast of Diwali, he decapitated them with his stick, which was converted into a sword by his patron goddess.

Probably the fame of the Gond rulers of Garha-Mandla first stirred him and his fellow Gonds to

[1] There is a local tradition, which makes Jatba a descendant of Sarbasha—a Gond King of Garha, who conquered Deogarh.

DEOGARH, NAGARKHARA

thoughts of an independent kingdom. Whatever it may have been, the great step was taken on a day when, in a State procession Jatba, at the suggestion of the goddess, vaulted on to the back of the royal elephant and most treacherously and savagely slew his royal masters.

Thus began the reign of Jatba. It is to him, tradition has it, that the city of Deogarh, with its famous fortress, mainly owes its existence. Here for over three centuries Gond Rajahs ruled, not only dominating the surrounding hilly country, but extending their influence away south into the plain country as far as the modern city of Nagpur, so that at one time this part of Gondwana was known as Deogarh above and Deogarh below the ghats. Under the fostering care of Jatba the kingdom of Deogarh steadily grew and the regions round Seoni and Chappara were in due time made part of it.

It might have been thought that the very remoteness of its position would have saved Deogarh from the notice of the Moghul Emperors. This, however, was not the case. Close to it, not more than fifty or sixty miles away, stood Kherla, the capital of another Gond kingdom. And Kherla lay not far from the route down which the Moslem armies passed from Northern India into the Berars and Deccan. During one of their campaigns the attention of the Delhi Emperor was called to the hill fortress of Deogarh, and in due time Jatba's kingdom passed under some kind of

Moghul suzerainty. It is said that the Emperor Akbar visited Deogarh during Jatba's reign, and that Jatba afterwards paid a return visit to Delhi.

After Jatba's death the kingdom was ruled well and wisely by his son and grandson, and continued to grow. Greatest of all of Jatba's descendants, however, was Bakt Buland. Few, if any, of the Gond princes of Gondwana were quite as famous as he was. There is a tradition that, when a young man, Bakt Buland visited the Moghul Court at Delhi and held some post in the Court. There his gallantry and courage so charmed the Emperor, that Aurangzeb bestowed upon the Prince his name or title of Bakt Buland, "one of great respect."

During his stay in Delhi, whether impressed by the truths of the Mohammedan religion, or for motives of political expediency, Bakt Buland embraced Islam, though there is not the slightest evidence that he used his influence on his return to Gondwana to induce his subjects to forsake their "Animism" for this faith. Indeed, it is an interesting fact that while Bakt Buland's successors have continued to be Moslems to the present day, the fact that they are Mohammedans has never prevented them from marrying into Gond families, and being received everywhere by their subjects as pure Gonds. When, for example, the present Gond Rajah, now a pensioner of Government, married, the bride was an ordinary Gond girl, and

DEOGARH, THE RUINED THRONE

the ceremonies took place at Deogarh according to the regular Gond rites. Only when all the customs of his fathers had been fulfilled was the bride received into the Mohammedan faith.

But Bakt Buland was not content to remain always the humble vassal of the Moghul Emperor. When in later life the Moslem kingdoms of the Deccan were at war with one another, and Moghul power was declining, Bakt Buland, following the customs of his ancestors, began a systematic course of plunder in the Moslem territories and even annexed Kherla. So serious were his depredations that they were in due course brought to the notice of Aurangzeb. As on enquiry it was proved beyond doubt that Bakt Buland's offences had been great, an Imperial order was issued by which he was deprived of his fair sounding title, and his name changed to Nigun Bakt, "Of mean fortune."

We should be doing injustice to the memory of Bakt Buland if we allowed our readers to think that his courage and prowess were exhibited in nothing greater than the occupations of a brigand. Ever ready to defend what he considered a just cause, and to stand by his Gond fellow-countrymen, he readily responded to the cry for help which came to him from Garha-Mandla, when the Rajah, Narind Shah, was sore pressed by the rebellion of two Pathan feudatory chieftains. Indeed, so prompt and so effective was the assistance then rendered by Bakt Buland to the Northern Gond

Rajah, that the rebellion was speedily put an end to, and the two Pathan chieftains were overpowered and slain.

It is to Bakt Buland that the beginnings of Nagpur, the modern capital of the Central Provinces, may first be traced. During his reign, the rich lands to the south of Deogarh, between the Wainganga and Kanhan rivers, were steadily developed. Hindu and Mohammedan cultivators were encouraged to settle in them on equal terms with Gonds, until this region became most prosperous.

On the death of Bakt Buland, his son, Chand Sultan, succeeded him, and, unlike so many Indian princes, carried on vigorously the work which his father had begun. During his reign Nagpur was raised to the dignity of a walled city, and traces of its old walls and gates, as well as some of its Gond buildings, are still to be seen in the modern city.

Then after days of prosperity came days of internal strife and dissension within the family of the ruling chief, until a fatal day dawned when the Marathas in Berar were invited by the Gond rulers to assist them in healing their internal quarrels—and with this came the end, and the house of Jatba passed away, to give place for a hundred years to Maratha rule.

To-day, almost under the shadow of the fort of Sitabaldi, at Nagpur, are the residences of two Rajahs, the one a descendant of Jatba, and the

DEOGARH, TOMB OF GOND KINGS

other a descendant of the Bhonsla who deposed the Gond dynasty, both Rajahs, Gond and Maratha alike, pensioners of the British Government; and away to the north, beneath the fortress of Deogarh, may be seen the tombs of the Gond kings of this Eastern Middle Kingdom, while in a place by itself stands the solitary tomb of Jatba, the founder of the line.

CHAPTER VI

KHERLA, AND THE WESTERN MIDDLE GOND KINGDOM

WITHIN a few miles of the pretty little station of Betul stands a conical hill from whose summit one gains a fine view of the surrounding country.

Around the base of this hill can still be seen large portions of the old walls, with their picturesque gates and massive bastions, which were called on over and over again in days of old to withstand fierce attacks of the Moslem. On the summit of the hill there stands a partially ruined citadel, in which more than once a last brave stand was made by its defenders.

Kherla, as this old fortress city is named, was for centuries a place from which various dynasties of kings ruled over the neighbouring country, and for a considerable period of this time Gond kings lived and ruled within its walls.

From many points of view the situation of Kherla was admirable. Standing in the heart of the plateau country of the Satpuras, more than 2,000 feet above sea-level, and not far from the source of the River Tapti, its open position was in marked contrast to the fortress city of Deogarh, where Jatba had built his capital. Kherla had, however, one fatal defect as compared with Deogarh. It was too near to the main highway which linked up Northern and Southern India.

FORTRESS OF KHERLA

KHERLA

If one may venture to take an illustration from sacred history, the position of Kherla was not unlike that of Samaria, whereas the position of Deogarh, shut away in hilly country, was somewhat like that of Jerusalem. And the varying histories of these two fortresses and kingdoms were, as might be expected, largely the outcome of their geographical position. For while the armies of Chaldea and Egypt, moving across the Holy Land, frequently turned aside to attack Samaria, leaving the rock-fortress of Jerusalem alone, so the Moslem armies, on their way to and from North and South India, passing by the great fortress of Asirgarh and across the Satpuras, constantly attacked Kherla, while Deogarh, fifty or sixty miles away in the heart of a hilly country, was left almost untouched.

The fortress of Kherla seems in the course of history, to have been little better than a shuttlecock between the greater powers which lay to the north and south of it. Desired as a strong outpost both by the Moslem kings to the south, and the Moslem princes who ruled in Mandu to the north, it was never for long left undisturbed. Constantly was it drawn into contests, with which it had little concern, and from which it could reap no benefit.

Long before the period of Gond rule, and before the Moslem invader moved southward, a Rajput dynasty had established itself at Kherla. These Rajputs were apparently great builders, and to

4—(3551)

them is ascribed the first building of the fortress of Kherla. To Jaitpal in particular, the last and most distinguished of this line of rulers, is ascribed much of the beauty and strength of the fortress.

Though a Hindu by religion, while carrying out his building schemes, he was guilty of a grave act of impiety, which hastened the end of his rule. In great straits for labour, he pressed into his service 300 Sadhus or "holy men." Those who know how these "beggar saints" are regarded in India can fully understand how such an act was regarded. Rumours of the hardships to which these "holy men" were subjected having reached Benares, the holy city of the Hindus, the feelings of that city were deeply moved. Mukund Raj, a Brahman of repute, was at once despatched to rebuke Jaitpal for his impiety, and to rescue the Sadhus from his unholy hands. As, however, Jaitpal was obdurate, Mukund Raj appears to have solved the problem by making the pickaxes of the Sadhus do their work, without the Sadhus' hands touching them!

Jaitpal was succeeded by Narsingh Rai, who was the first Gond king to rule in Kherla. It is, however, open to question whether he was a pure Gond, as one tradition has it that he was the son of a marriage between a Rajput father and a Gond mother. His date seems to have been somewhat late in the fourteenth century. During his reign the kingdom of Kherla stretched away in a

FORTRESS OF ASIRGARH

westerly direction into the hill country north of Berar, embracing the celebrated fortress of Gawalgarh near Chikalda.

His reign was one of constant warfare. At one period we see him at war with the Moslem ruler of Ellichpur in Berar. At another he is at war with the northern kingdom of Malwa. Feroz Shah, the Moslem King of Ellichpur, was the first to invade his country. On that occasion, he laid siege to Kherla, and actually captured Narsingh Rai's eldest son. Then for a short time the tables were turned, and Ellichpur was besieged by Narsingh Rai. This good fortune did not, however, last for long, and shortly afterwards Narsingh Rai and his army were compelled to capitulate at Ellichpur. Then it was that Feroz Shah, with a view to winning the Gond prince over to his side, forgave him magnanimously, presented him with a robe of honour, and took one of his daughters into the royal harem.

After this a fresh page in Narsingh Rai's chequered history was opened, and we see the Gond prince an ally of the Moslem king of Ellichpur, and in consequence an object of the inveterate hostility of Hoshang, Moslem king of Malwa. More than once Kherla was invested by this famous warrior from Mandu, who swore to take it because Narsingh Rai had refused his alliance. Then again for a brief period the wheel of fortune turned, and Narsingh Rai pursued the army of Hoshang when retreating from an unsuccessful invasion of the Deccan across his hilly country, and cut it in pieces.

The next act of the drama took place when the Ellichpur king Ahmed Shah, Narsingh Rai's ally, was campaigning far away in Gujerat. Hoshang then seized his opportunity, and attacked his old enemy with renewed hatred and violence. In the battle which ensued, Narsingh fell, and Kherla passed into the hands of Hoshang. After this tragic event Kherla remained for a time in Hoshang's hands, until the Ellichpur king again wrested it from his grasp, and incorporated it in the Moghul empire. After this Kherla became for a time the headquarters of a Mohammedan governor, and was under the Subah of Ellichpur. With the decline of Moghul influence, however, in the Deccan, Kherla passed into the hands of Bakt Buland, the famous Gond ruler of Deogarh, and from that time onwards it remained under Gond rulers until the rise of the Maratha power. With this brief account of it we must unfortunately be content. Unlike the other Gond kingdoms of Gondwana, almost no records of its Gond rulers have been preserved for us.

Not in such a region as Kherla could Gond rule develop naturally along its own lines. Its true sphere was in remote places like Deogarh and Chanda, where Moslem armies seldom came, and where king and people could live their lives free from fears of the invader.

VIEW FROM ASIRGARH

CHAPTER VII

THE SOUTHERN GOND KINGDOM

INDIA has been described as the "Land of Surprises," and the first sight of Chanda is to most people a real surprise. Who would expect to find such a charming little city, hidden away in the heart of the jungles. There it has stood for the last five centuries with its beautiful crenelated walls and battlements which have suffered surprisingly little from time's or man's rough hands. Unlike the Gond capitals of Deogarh, Kherla, and Chauragarh, Chanda stands in the open plains more than 100 miles to the south of the Satpuras. If, as is probable, the original home of the Gond race was in the forest country of the Deccan, the Gonds in the Chanda district are much nearer the rock from which they were hewn than are the Gonds away to the north in the Satpuras.

Centuries before Khandkia Ballal Shah laid the foundations of the city of Chanda, other dynasties of kings had ruled in this part of India. There had been, in this neighbourhood, in very early days, a great Hindu city Bhadravati, dedicated to Bhadra (a name for the god Shiva), the capital of the Vakataka kings. These kings ruled over a wide stretch of country from the Godavary to the Mahanadi, and northwards to the Mahadeo range of the Satpuras. Then when Buddhism penetrated into the heart of India, and for a time secured the faith and devotion of the more highly cultured Indians, the city of Kosala eclipsed the glory of Bhadravati.

How famous Kosala was may be seen from the description which Hiuen Tsang—a Chinese Buddhist pilgrim—thought fit to give of it when writing in A.D. 639. "One hundred monasteries are here and ten thousand Buddhist priests are among its inhabitants." But Buddhism, with its high morality and philosophy of despair, never won the soul of the peoples of India, and in due course Kosala, and its Buddhist rulers, faded away, to be replaced by the Manas or Nagvansi (snake worshippers !) kings of Wairagarh.

It was at this period that visions of rule first dawned amongst the head-men of the Gond tribes. Tradition has it that it was to one man, Kol Bhil, whose name is a curious combination of the names of two other aboriginal races, that the Southern Gonds owe the beginnings of their rule. A man of great strength and wisdom, he first welded the Gond tribes together, and taught them the elements of civilisation. It is, however, with Bhim Ballal Singh that the Southern Gond dynasty actually begins. His capital was at Sirpur, on the right bank of the Wardha river, and his chief stronghold was the fortress of Manikgarh, in the hills behind Sirpur. For the first eight generations these Southern Gond kings reigned at Sirpur, in the modern State of Hyderabad.

Conspicuous amongst these rulers was Hir Singh, the grandson of Bhim Ballal Singh. Brave in war, and wise in administration, he was the first to persuade his wild fellow-countrymen to cultivate the land. To him is attributed something like a rudimentary land-revenue system. In the time of his grandson, Dinkar Singh, the culture of the Gond court improved. Though a self-indulgent character, he was in some respects more enlightened than his predecessors. Gond bards flocked to his capital at Sirpur and pundits, acquainted with Marathi, were encouraged to settle there.

On his death his son Ram Singh succeeded him. Of him it is written—

"Just and truthful in his intercourse with his subjects, and daring and successful as a soldier, Ram Singh governed the kingdom righteously and enlarged its bounds. To increase its security he erected several hill-forts on the south-west, and maintained a chosen band of warriors called 'Tarvels.' These men had eaten the 'taru' (a rare orchid) with certain ceremonial observances, and were supposed to be invulnerable. To each of his Tarvels the King made grants of land."

Ram Singh was succeeded by his son Surja Ballal Singh, who is one of the most romantic figures of old Gondwana. Handsome in person, and a lover of adventure, he began his princely career by some years of wandering. After visiting Benares, the holy city of Hinduism, he journeyed to Lucknow, where he devoted himself to the study of war and song. His troubadour-like existence in Oudh, however, was cut short in a rather unpleasant manner. The looting propensities of his Gond escort having reached the ears of the Emperor at Delhi, orders went out for the Gond prince's arrest. This was no easy matter, as his brave Tarvels were ever watchful of their master, and on several occasions proved more than a match for the imperial troops, who were sent from Delhi to arrest him. One day, however, when wandering near Lucknow, without his escort, Ballal Singh was captured, and carried off to Delhi, where he was kept in close confinement. Horrified at the capture of their brave prince, his escort of Tarvels hastened back to Gondwana to break the evil tidings at the Gond capital of Sirpur. Then it was that the " tocsin " resounded throughout the forest lands of Chanda, and the Tarvels were summoned by Jarba, the regent, to come speedily to the rescue of Ballal Singh.

Meanwhile things had taken a turn for the better with Surja Ballal Singh. As he wiled away the weary hours of his captivity in song, it fell out one day that the Emperor's lovely daughter passing by that part of the palace where he was confined, heard him singing. Desirous of seeing the prince

PATHANPURA GATE, CHANDA

who could sing so well, she persuaded the Emperor to send for him. The result of this interview was just what Ballal Singh must have desired. Struck by his princely bearing the Emperor enquired whether Ballal Singh could fight as well as sing. On the Gond prince replying that he only longed for an opportunity of showing his skill in battle, the Emperor allotted to him the difficult task of subduing the fortress of Mohan Singh which his own generals had failed to take. This Rajput prince had incurred the Emperor's displeasure by refusing to give his beautiful daughter to the imperial harem.

Hardly had Ballal Singh accepted this honourable task, and before he had time to start for Gondwana, where he was about to raise an army of Gonds, there appeared before the gates of Delhi the Gond regent Jarba and an army of Tarvels and other Gonds, bent on the rescue of their prince. On learning the changed condition of affairs, and that their prince was now a commander in the Moslem armies, Jarba gladly agreed to accompany the expedition.

Ten thousand picked soldiers from the imperial troops were added to the force, and Ballal Singh was soon on his way to the rebellious State. The campaign was a brief and successful one. The Tarvels, under the leadership of their prince, performed miracles of valour, stormed the fortress, slew the Rajah, and captured his widow and daughter.

Then follows the romance of the story. The beautiful widow implored the chivalrous Surja Ballal Singh to save her and her daughter from the imperial harem, and he, overcome by her charms, rashly undertook to do so. His task was by no means an easy one, but Surja Ballal Singh eventually devised a plan by which he succeeded in deceiving the Emperor and acquiring the ladies for himself.

A rumour was started by his orders among his troops, that his eldest son—a beautiful boy—had just arrived in camp. Disguising the beautiful young Rajputni princess in boy's dress, he placed her on the state elephant on which he himself rode triumphantly into Delhi. Proceeding to the imperial palace he announced his arrival, and craved the audience of the Emperor. The Emperor seated on his throne in the Diwan-i-Khass, welcomed the victorious prince, and taking the beautiful child on his knee addressed him as his dear child. Then turning to Ballal Singh he asked of him: "Where, O Prince, is the fruit of thy victory?" "Your Majesty holds her in your lap," replied the Gond prince, "and as you have called her 'Your dear child' she can be nothing else to you."

What the Emperor really felt about this trick which Surja Ballal Singh had played on him we are not told. His honour, however, was now involved, and he at once renounced all claim to the Rajput ladies, who later on accompanied the

Gond prince to his capital at Sirpur. It speaks well for an autocrat like the Emperor of Delhi that in spite of this act of deception he was ready to confer on Surja Ballal Singh a dress of honour as a reward for his bravery. The title of "Sher Shah" was also conferred on him, so that after his return from Delhi he was no longer known as Surja Ballal Singh, but as Sher Shah Ballal Shah.

Readers of Gond records cannot fail to be struck by the fact that while the earlier rulers of the Northern and Southern Gond dynasties are styled "Singh" (the Rajput title for a ruler), the later rulers are styled "Shah," an abbreviated form of Padishah, the Moslem term for a ruler. Doubtless the change of title merely marked the decline of early Rajput influence, and the ascendency of the Moghul power.

CHAPTER VIII

CHANDA, AND THE SOUTHERN GOND KINGDOM

ON the death of the heroic Surja, his son Khandkia Ballal Shah came to the throne. Suffering constantly from ill-health, it seemed hardly possible that his reign would add any lustre to the southern house of Gond kings. And yet, strange though it may seem, it was this very ill-health of their ruler which was destined to bring about a change, which did so much to strengthen the position of the Southern Gond kingdom.

Khandkia's queen was a woman of more than ordinary discernment and decision of character. In her anxiety for his health she urged him to abandon the home of his ancestors at Sirpur, and to seek a healthier and more secure capital on the opposite side of the Wardha river. Acting on her advice, the Gond king moved his capital to a site on the high banks of the left bank of the Wardha river which still bears his name. There he built the picturesque fortress of Ballarshah—now partly in ruins—which commands a splendid view of the river and a wide sweep of Deccan country.

Still suffering from his disease, he spent much of his time in the saddle, exploring the surrounding country, and hunting its game. It was while engaged on one of his hunting expeditions that the event occurred which led to the founding of the city of Chanda. Riding one day some ten miles from Ballarshah, he became extremely thirsty, and while walking his horse up the dry bed of a small river, to his great joy discovered a small pool of water in its rocky bed. Dismounting he greedily drank the cool water, and bathed his face and hands in the pool. That night on his return to Ballarshah, he slept as he had not slept for years. In the morning when he awoke his queen noticed that the swellings and tumours which had disfigured his handsome face and body for some years had almost vanished. In her delight she questioned him closely about the pool in which he had bathed, and being convinced that there was more in it than ordinary water, she implored Ballal Shah to take her over to it that very morning.

On reaching the spot orders were at once given to have all the grass and jungle removed from around the pool, when, to the wonder and delight of the king and queen, as well as to the assembled court, five deep footprints of the sacred cow were seen in the solid rock, each filled with an unfailing supply of water. Further enquiry made it clear that this spot was none other than the resting-place of the great god Achaleshwar, "The Immovable One."

Further bathing in its sacred waters soon restored the king to complete health, and removed all his bodily disfigurements. Not long afterwards, to confirm this great discovery, the god Achaleshwar appeared in a night vision to the happy king. Then again the good sense of his queen stood Khandkia Ballal Shah in good stead. Possessed of a genius for taking hints from either gods or men, she made it quite clear to the king that the god Achaleshwar expected him to build a temple over the sacred pools in his honour. Plans of the temple were speedily prepared, stone was quarried, the foundations were laid with due ceremony, and before many months the temple of Achaleshwar was rising from the ground, a temple which still stands, after 500 years, in memory of Khandkia Ballal Shah's restoration to health and happiness.

While this temple was in process of construction, another event occurred which was to lead to the founding of the city of Chanda. It was the king's custom to ride over from Ballarshah from time to time to see how the work at the temple progressed. On his rides he was invariably accompanied by a favourite dog. One day when riding back to Ballarshah, and while close to the temple, a hare darted out of a bush, and strange to relate began to chase his dog. The dog fled in wild terror with the hare in close pursuit. Astonished at the sight, the king followed the chase as closely as he could. At times, with a view of shaking off his pursuer, the dog ran in wide circles, while the hare took a shorter and

CHANDA, CITY WALLS WITH ACHALESHWAR TEMPLE

more zigzag course. On one occasion the hare actually closed with the dog, only to be quickly shaken off. And so the race continued until both the animals were nearly exhausted. Then when they were approaching the place where the race had begun, after a circular chase of nearly seven miles, the dog in wild desperation turned on the hare, and after a sharp struggle killed it.

Approaching the dead hare, the Gond Rajah observed for the first time that on its forehead was a strange white mark or "tika." Full of his strange adventure he rode back to Ballarshah to tell the story to his sympathetic queen. Again her genius penetrated into the inner meaning of this mysterious occurrence. It was clearly an omen sent by the gods that Khandkia Ballal Shah was again to change his capital, and build a fortified city around the temple of Achaleshwar. The chase was but the god's own method of town-planning. The walls of the city must be built over the tracks of the sacred hare—strong bastions must be built at the places where the dog had made his circular detour—and special fortifications would be needed where the hare had closed with the dog, and also where the dog had slain the hare; for these would always be danger zones in the new city. Thus was begun the city of Chanda, or Chandrapur, which, according to some, derives its name from the moon, and according to others from the white spot on the hare's forehead.

Khandkia Ballal Shah was succeeded by his son Hir Shah, in whose reign the country prospered. Like his remote ancestor, Hir Singh of Sirpur, his mind was bent on the improvement of agriculture in South Gondwana. Calling the trusty Tarvels to a banquet, he urged on them the duty of clearing and cultivating the lands which his grandfather had bestowed on them. To everyone who cleared his lands of forest and jungle, was offered the rights of ownership, whereas those who through laziness and apathy refused to do so, were duly warned that their lands would be confiscated. Nor was Hir Shah content with merely issuing orders on these subjects. From time to time it was his custom to tour throughout his wild State, for the purpose of seeing for himself how his orders had been obeyed. Boundaries were then marked out, and "sanads," or rights of tenure, were formally bestowed on worthy landholders. Special rewards also were given to those who had constructed tanks on their property—and those who had made irrigation channels or canals were often given all the land which their waters reached.

In this way much of the wild country was brought under cultivation, and numbers of the migratory Gonds were drawn into the quiet life of the agriculturist. It is to Hir Shah in particular that the Chanda district owes so many of its splendid tanks.

Once a year all landowners appeared before

the Rajah at Chanda to pay their rents and exhibit their ploughs and other field implements. By this means a rough calculation of the value of their property was made.

In Hir Shah's reign the massive gates of Chanda, with their quaint emblem of Gond sovereignty—" the elephant helpless in the grasp of a gigantic tiger," which resembled the mastodon of prehistoric days, were completed. To him also belongs the honour of building the citadel and the palace, parts of which still remain, though degraded to the less noble uses of a jail and police station! Of Hir Shah it is specially recorded that he paid tribute to no foreign king, so that any over-lordship on the part of the Bahmani kings of the Deccan—which had hitherto existed—from his time passed away.

On his death his two sons Bhuma and Lokba jointly ruled the kingdom, according to a scheme laid down by their father. Fortunately no jealousy or rival ambitions were felt by either of them. Those were merry days in Chanda, like the days of Good Queen Bess in England. In the summer season the various Gond chieftains and headmen waited on their princes, with bodies painted in divers colours, and adorned with various ornaments, such as peacocks' feathers, beetles' wings, tiger and panther skins, and the horns of the young bison. Each headman brought with him specimens of the various products found on his estate, both animal and vegetable, and the festivities concluded with a great banquet at the royal palace.

There was a pleasing diversity among these old Gond rulers of Chanda. Some were stern warriors, full of ambition to extend their territories; while others were more peacefully inclined, who won their triumphs in the development of the resources of their forests and jungles.

Karn Shah, the grandson of Hir Shah, belonged, however, to another and less common type of ruler. Thoughtful and religious, he was from the first strongly attracted to the Hindu religion. A lover of its sacred books, Brahmans and Pandits soon flocked to his kingdom, and were rewarded with fields and villages free of rent. Lingas of Mahadeo were set up in many places, new temples built and old temples restored. Justice, too, was administered as never before. Before his days—so legend has it—no king in South Gondwana ever dreamt of interfering in the disputes of his subjects, and every man was his own judge and high-executioner. If anyone had appealed to the king for justice when their relations had been murdered, the king had but one reply, "Slay your enemy." In Karn Shah's days this state of things was no longer tolerated. Justice was evenly administered, and habitual offenders were banished from the State. Falsehood and perjury were punished with the utmost severity, and men dwelt securely under the shadow of their vines and fig-trees.

Seldom is any mention made of these jungle kingdoms in the annals of the Imperial Court at Delhi, but so prosperous and important had Southern Gondwana become at this period that in the Ain-i-Akbari, or Chronicles of Akbar, it is recorded of Babaji Ballal Shah, Karn Shah's son, "that he paid no tribute to Delhi, and possessed an army of 10,000 cavalry and 40,000 infantry." In his reign the city of Wairagarh—the capital of their hereditary foes—was added to the kingdom of Chanda.

As one endeavours to piece together the fragmentary accounts which we possess of the four kingdoms of old Gondwana, one cannot help asking the question as to the connection, if any, which existed between them. Were they friends and allies, or in the usual condition of suspicion and hostility which was characteristic of most Indian States at that period?

It certainly seems as if, during one period, the kingdom of Chanda penetrated into the Satpura country, and encroached very considerably on the kingdom of Deogarh. On the other hand, our scant records tell us of but one war waged between the houses of Chanda and Deogarh, and that as a consequence of an unhappy marriage.

At the time of this marriage between the ruling houses of these two kingdoms both were at the height of prosperity, and bound to one another by some kind of treaty. Abul-l-Fazl speaks of the strength of Deogarh as then being very considerable, "fifty thousand foot, and two thousand cavalry and one hundred elephants." We have already seen what the strength of Chanda was.

The quarrel arose in the following manner: Bir Shah, one of the most distinguished princes of Chanda, had given his daughter to Durgpal, a prince of the royal house of Deogarh. Durgpal, who most probably had never seen the princess till the day of his marriage, seems to have taken a violent dislike to his bride, and to have insulted her in some inexcusable way. Bir Shah in wild anger vowed that he would never rest till he had placed the head of the miscreant Durgpal on the top of the shrine of the great goddess Kali at Chanda.

A bloody battle ensued, and in its earlier stages everything went well with the Moslem Gond king of Deogarh. Bir Shah was on the point of being captured, when drawing the sacred sword of his house, and with a loud voice invoking the aid of Maha Kali, he rushed on Durgpal, and with one blow deprived his son-in-law of his head. After the death of their prince the army of Deogarh lost heart and fled, and Bir Shah returned with his triumphant army to Chanda. And to-day, high up on the roof of the lofty temple of Maha Kali, which lies outside the city walls of Chanda on its southern side, one may see a head carved in stone gazing away northwards to Deogarh, which recalls the story of the unfortunate Durgpal.

MAHA KALI TEMPLE, CHANDA

Bir Shah's own end was even more tragic than that of his son-in-law. It came to him on the day of his second marriage. There is an old Indian custom that part of the bridegroom's duty on the marriage day is to fetch the bride from her father's house to his own. For some years there had been at Bir Shah's court a Rajput named Hiraman, renowned for his skill at arms and believed to be the possessor of a magic sword. More than once Bir Shah had asked this rather mysterious person to reveal to him the secret of his sword, but to no purpose. And for the last time on this happy day, before the royal procession set out to the bride's house, he again asked him, half in banter, to explain to him the secret. Hitherto silent and sullen, Hiraman suddenly burst forth into a fierce passion, and before the courtiers could intervene, killed the king, and then killed himself. So perished Bir Shah, one of the bravest and best of the Gond kings of Chanda. And to mark the deep sense of loss at his tragic death, the noblest of all the tombs in Chanda was raised over his grave, close to the temple of Achaleshwar.

And now we must draw our tale of the Gond kings of Chanda to an end. Of them we know far more than of the other kings. Only in the days of Sangram Shah and Durgavati, and in the days of Bakt Buland, did the Gond kingdoms of Northern Garha-Mandla, and Deogarh, at all rival the greatness of the southern house. Unlike the other Gond kingdoms, the house of Chanda seems to have had a long succession of good and intelligent rulers, who resisted the natural temptations to inner strife and intrigue, which, as we have already seen, brought destruction to the other kingdoms. Indeed, so famous for wisdom and uprightness was Ram Shah, one of the last kings of Chanda, that it is reported of him that when Raghuji Bhonsla, the Maratha leader, visited Chanda, with a view to seeking a pretext for a quarrel, he ended his visit by almost worshipping him as a god.

" Well would it have been," so Canon Wood writes in his article on Chanda, " if the fast failing thread of the Gond rule had been severed at Ram Shah's death."

For Ram Shah's son and successor, Nilkanth Shah, was an evil and cruel ruler, who dismissed his father's most trustworthy councillors, ground down his subjects, and interfered foolishly and needlessly in the political disputes of Deogarh. And all the time the Maratha foe was but waiting for his opportunity, and when he again approached the gates of the royal city of Chanda, it was not by force of arms, but by the treachery of a discontented people, that he triumphed.

Certainly the achievements of the southern house of Gondwana were quite remarkable. " Originally but petty chiefs of a savage tribe, they spread their kingdom over a wide stretch of country, reclaiming much of the forest land, peopling them with a prosperous people, and keeping their country free from the foreign invader. And when at length they passed away, they left a well-governed kingdom, prosperous to a point which has not since been reached."

CHAPTER IX

NAGPUR

THE MARATHA PERIOD, 1743–1853

THE map of ancient India differed a good deal from its map to-day. The country to the south of Nerbudda was roughly divided ethnographically by Hindu geographers into five parts: "Draved" on the extreme south, "Telingana" and the "Carnatic" in the centre, "Gondwana" to the north of Telingana, and "Maharasthra" to the north of the Carnatic.

Maharasthra was the home of the Marathas. From it they took their name. It was a large tract of country, which in its northern portion included some of the Satpura hill country, while its south-western portion extended along the coast line as far as Goa.

Risley, in his *Peoples of India*, seems to think that the Maratha race owes its origin to an ancient Scythian invasion of India. These Scythian invaders intermarried largely with the Dravidian races, whom they conquered, and settled down to a life, partly agricultural, but chiefly pastoral. Though Hindus in religion, and speaking a language which is derived from Sanskrit, the Marathas retain special customs of their own, and still exhibit many marked features of character and appearance, which separate them from the other peoples of India.

Before the Mohammedan invasions of India, Maharasthra was divided into States of varying size and importance, most of them small. Unlike Gondwana, it lay on the direct route between Northern and Southern India, and soon passed under Mohammedan domination. During the earlier days of Mohammedan rule in the territories south of the Nerbudda, and for long years after the Bahmani revolt from Delhi, the Marathas were content to live under what was to them an alien rule. Many of them filled various offices of distinction in Moslem States. When, however, the Bahmani dynasty, after a century and a half of rule, broke up into the five, and afterwards three, Moslem kingdoms of the Deccan; when southern Moslems were divided against their brethren, and the Moghul emperors of Delhi with their varying and generally aggressive policy, only added to the political unrest of the country, the first movement towards an independent national rule awoke amongst the Marathas. They had learnt from their conquerors how to rule and how to fight, and they began to turn their lessons to account. Little did the Moghul Emperor Aurungzeb realise when he contemptuously styled the Maratha leader Sivaji "a mountain rat," that the Maratha forces which this remarkable man was beginning to arouse would within a century be around his capital, Delhi, and at the battle of

Panipat be even threatening the supremacy of his empire.

It is not my intention to touch on the general history of the Marathas.

It is sufficient for our purpose to trace briefly the connection of the Maratha kingdoms with the old Gond kingdoms of the Central Provinces.

More than two generations had passed since Sivaji had been gathered to his fathers, before the Marathas finally established their rule in old Gondwana. It is always a dangerous experiment to summon outside help to settle internal quarrels. Those who are invited have an unpleasant way of staying on, when their stay is no longer welcome. Chand Sultan's widow was naturally anxious about her son Burhan Shah's succession to his father's throne, and was justly indignant at the usurpation of Wali Shah, a natural son of the great Bakt Buland. She and her advisers, however, can hardly have realised the character of those from whom they sought help. Not that Raghuji Bhonsla, the Maratha ruler of Berar to whom she appealed, treated her and the Gond kingdom badly, for it is clear that he showed them far more consideration than many of his compatriots would have done. His response to the first cry for help was merely to dispossess the usurper, and to assist in putting Burhan Shah on his throne. When he had done this, he retired to his capital at Ellichpur in Berar.

But Burhan Shah was a poor creature, and

almost immediately after his trouble with Wali Shah, was involved in strife with one of his own brothers, Akbar Shah. Those were evil days in Gondwana. Gond fought against Gond, and on one occasion no less than 12,000 Gonds were massacred in cold blood by Akbar Shah. Again Raghuji was summoned, and this time he decided to stay. Burhan Shah was obviously too weak to keep order over the fair lands which the genius and courage of his grandfather, Bakt Buland, had bequeathed to him, and so Raghuji made up his mind to take the reins of government out of the hands of the feeble Gond Rajah. Even then, however, he showed no harshness to him, and treated him with an outward show of respect. Burhan Shah remained the nominal ruler of the kingdom to the end of his days and, what is more, received a fixed share of the revenues of his country. Thus in this bloodless fashion the Maratha began his rule over the Central Provinces.

Before, however, we proceed further, it may be well to say a word or two about this Maratha family of Bhonslas, who ruled over Gondwana for nearly one hundred years. The founder of their family was Mudhoji Patel of Deor, a small State in the Bombay Presidency. Mudhoji had been a distinguished cavalry leader in the armies of Sivaji. His son Parsoji, as a reward for military service in the early Maratha wars, was made governor of Berar, the country which lay on the borders of Gondwana, with the right of collecting

"Chauth" or revenue in that country. Parsoji was in due course succeeded by his nephew, the above-mentioned Raghuji, who was the first Maratha ruler of Nagpur. Of Raghuji it has been said "he was a perfect type of a Maratha ruler. He saw in the troubles of others only an opening for his own ambition and did not require a further pretext for plunder and invasion."

No sooner did Raghuji find himself established in Nagpur than he at once developed his plans for conquering all the surrounding country. The city of Chanda, the capital of the Southern Gond kingdom, was delivered up to him by treachery in 1749. Maratha rule spread rapidly in a northern direction, and the fate of Chanda soon overtook Kherla. Before Raghuji's death, in 1755, much of the country between the Godavery and the Nerbudda, and from the Bay of Bengal to the extreme east of Berar, was paying tribute or "Chauth"—"25 per cent. of the land tax"—to this Maratha ruler.

During Raghuji's time a great change passed over the southern portion of the Central Provinces. Large numbers of Kumbhis (the cultivating class of Marathas) and of other Maratha tribes poured into the Nagpur country. Gondi, the old language, ceased to be spoken, and Marathi took its place. And with the change the old Gond population withdrew more and more into the wilder parts of the country.

The early Maratha rulers of Nagpur were

NAGPUR—FORT OF SITABALDI

soldiers and adventurers rather than administrators. Fighting was the main business of their lives. Their morality was on a par with that of the modern German militarists ; everything was right which advanced what they regarded as their own interests, or the interests of their State.

Raghuji's son, Janoji, who succeeded him, though a popular ruler, and careful in the observance of his religious and secular duties, was entirely devoid of honour in his dealings with other States, whether compatriot Marathas or Moslem. On one occasion we see him accepting a huge bribe from the Nizam, his traditional foe, a Moslem, and betraying in the most shameful way his compatriot, the young Peshwa. His treachery, however, was brought home to him later on in his reign, in 1765, when the enraged Peshwa, joining hands with the Nizam, sacked and burnt Janoji's capital at Nagpur.

After Janoji's death in 1770, the kingdom of Nagpur was again plunged into civil war over the question of his successor. For two years a bitter struggle went on between his two sons, Sabaji and Mudhoji, till on a memorable day at Panchgaon, twelve miles south of Nagpur, just as victory was in Sabaji's hands, the latter fell by the hand of his brother Mudhoji.

During his Regency (for Mudhoji merely acted as Regent for his son Raghuji) the East India Company entered for the first time into treaty relationships with the Maratha kingdom of Nagpur, which, on account of the Maratha annexation of Orissa, had come into close contact with British territories in Bengal.

Hitherto the Northern Gond kingdom of Garha-Mandla had been regarded as but part of the Peshwa's dominions and was ruled from Poona. In 1785, however, it was definitely added to the kingdom of Nagpur by a treaty in which Mudhoji agreed to pay twenty-seven lakhs into the treasury at Poona. Mudhoji was, on the whole, a sensible ruler, and before his death in 1788 was able to hand over a tranquil and fairly prosperous State to his son Raghuji.

At the time of Raghuji II's accession, the kingdom of Nagpur embraced practically the whole of the present Central Provinces with Berar, the province of Orissa, and some of the Chota Nagpur States. Its annual revenue was estimated at nearly one million pounds. Its army consisted of 18,000 cavalry, a strong feature in all Maratha armies, with 25,000 infantry and 4,000 Arabs. The artillery was considerable, and included about ninety guns. It is interesting to note, however, that Raghuji's army was recruited for the most part outside Gondwana, the cavalry coming from Poona, and its neighbourhood, and the infantry from the fighting races of Rajputana or Arabia.

Up to 1803 it is generally admitted that the administration of the southern part of Gondwana was not without its good points. Descended as they were from the yeomen class, the Bhonsla rulers of Nagpur favoured agriculture, and though rapacious, were seldom deliberately cruel. They believed, like all Oriental rulers, in the personal touch of the ruler, and their Rajah might be seen from time to time, in the early mornings, sitting on his throne in the Public Hall of Audience, which opened on the main street of Nagpur, with sword and shield beside him, discussing with his ministers and military captains, the different problems of his State. At such times he was ready to listen to the appeals and complaints of his subjects, a privilege very dear to the Oriental, who feels that more than half of his troubles have passed away if the " Sircar " gives ear to the voice of his complaint.

During the early period of Raghuji II's reign the links between the Nagpur State and the Bengal Government grew firmer, and in 1798 Mr. Colebrooke was appointed Resident at the Court of Raghuji. Well would it have been for Raghuji, if he had more fully realised the importance of keeping on good terms with the British and had not allowed himself to be drawn first into intrigue, and then into open hostility, against them.

Mr. Colebrooke had hardly been in Nagpur for two years when indications of a curious change in Raghuji's attitude became apparent to him. Secretly encouraged by the Peshwa, the nominal leader of the Maratha Confederacy, Raghuji collected an army, and threw in his lot with Scindhia, then our bitter foe.

Shortly after Scindhia's defeat at Assaye by the Duke of Wellington, then Sir Arthur Wellesley, a similar fate befell Raghuji, at Argaon, followed almost immediately by the loss of his great fortress of Gawalgarh, near Chikalda. Nothing remained then for Raghuji but to accept peace on any terms. Shorn of his territories in the Berars and Orissa, his revenue fell to nearly one-half of its former amount.

From this time onwards Raghuji's character steadily deteriorated. Adversity seems only to have embittered him. Determined to show as proud a front as ever to the world, he began to tax his unfortunate subjects unmercifully. Opening numbers of shops in the bazaar he compelled people to buy in them, while charging exorbitant prices. Soon he became known as the "Big Bania" or "Big Shopkeeper." Jealous and suspicious of everyone, he found no one ready to serve him. His unpaid army turned into bands of dacoits, who looted the country-side far and wide. For security against them the villagers even raised forts in their villages, remains of which may still be seen. Forty years after his death old men spoke pathetically of the misery of those days. "They sowed in sorrow with little hope of reaping. When they did reap, they buried their corn in the ground." And so when Raghuji II died, the kingdom of Nagpur was in a state of abject misery and poverty such as had never been seen in earlier Gond days.

Nor did the succeeding years bring much relief. Raghuji's son, Parsoji, was blind, paralysed, and shortly after his accession lost his reason. Mudhoji, a nephew of the late Rajah, was then appointed Regent. On his appointment things looked at first more hopeful. A new British Resident, Mr. Jenkins, succeeded Mr. Mountstuart Elphinstone, our second Resident, and it seemed as if Mudhoji, under his guidance and advice, was ready to do all in his power to improve the condition of his State. Owing to straitened finances the army was reduced, and on 28th May, 1816, a treaty of defensive alliance was signed, by which the British East India Company agreed to maintain six regiments of infantry with cavalry and artillery, while Parsoji was to pay 7½ lakhs (£75,000) annually for the upkeep of 2,000 cavalry and 2,000 footmen.

Thus matters stood at the beginning of 1817, when Mudhoji the Regent left Nagpur ostensibly to visit the Chanda portions of his territories. Hardly, however, had he left his palace when the Rajah was found dead in his bed poisoned, so it was afterwards proved, by the Regent's orders, and as Parsoji had no heir, and as no one was prepared to prove that Mudhoji was the murderer, he, as his next of kin, was appointed Rajah.

Then a complete change came over this unscrupulous ruler. Dropping all concealment he at once showed himself in his true colours. In spite of continued professions of friendship to Mr. Jenkins, he openly conspired with the other chieftains of the Maratha Confederacy, the Peshwa and Scindhia, to destroy British rule and influence in India. By November, 1817, affairs had assumed so grave an aspect that Mr. Jenkins felt it necessary to summon all available troops to his assistance at Nagpur.

Before they could reach him, however, Mudhoji, popularly known as "Appa Sahib," determined to strike his blow. As a preliminary step, and to show openly his contempt for the British, he invited Mr. Jenkins and his staff to witness in Durbar his investiture as a "Sunobut" or Commander-in-Chief in the Peshwa's army, the Peshwa being then at war with us.

It being now clear that open hostilities were inevitable, Colonel Hopetoun Scott with a brigade of two battalions of Madras troops, and four six-pounders, manned by Europeans of the Madras artillery, was ordered to move swiftly from the lines at Telinkheri, and to occupy the small hill of Sitabaldi which overlooks the city of Nagpur.

Hardly had our troops occupied Sitabaldi when Appa Sahib's attack began. The Maratha forces numbered fully 18,000 men, of whom nearly 4,000 were Arabs. Their artillery amounted to thirty-six guns. Against this army Mr. Jenkins had but 1,800 Madras infantry, and four guns!

The battle of Sitabaldi, as it is called, began as late in the day as six o'clock on the evening of

THE BATTLE OF SITABALDI, EXPLOSION OF TUMBRIL

the 26th of November. The hill from which it takes its name consists of two summits, connected by a narrow neck, the northern summit, about 300 feet high, being slightly lower than the southern. As the northern summit, however, commanded the native city, it was naturally of special importance. The surface of the hill being almost entirely of rock, our troops could do but little in the way of entrenchment. Three hundred of our troops were left to hold this lower hill, while most of the remainder under Colonel Scott took up a position on the higher eminence. Beneath this higher hill lay the old Residency with the Resident, his staff, and a few English ladies. Within the Residency grounds were 200 infantry, and a small body of Bengal cavalry under Captain Fitzgerald.

Over and over again during the night determined efforts were made by the Marathas to rush the northern hill. None of the attacks, however, were quite successful, though pressed with great energy, and with heavy losses on both sides. When, however, morning broke, on 27th November, the position was absolutely desperate. Though reinforced more than once during the night, the numbers of defenders on the lower hill had dwindled to an alarming extent. Indeed, at nine o'clock in the morning it seemed as if all must be over in an hour or two at most, as the Arab troops, after a tremendous onslaught, favoured by the explosion of one of our small gunpowder tumbrils, gained the summit of the lower hill, overpowered our sepoys, and turned our gun upon the higher hill. Simultaneously with this a body of the Maratha cavalry succeeded in forcing their way into the grounds of the Residency.

Then it was that the courage of one British officer saved the day. More than once during that eventful morning, Captain Fitzgerald had asked permission of his superior officer to charge, and had, as often, been prevented. Now when destruction seemed inevitable, he made his final request.

The reply to his last appeal, if Grant Duff's version of the story is to be accepted, was hardly an encouraging one. "Tell him to charge at his peril" (or "At the hazard of his commission"), was the message which reached him. "If only at the hazard of my commission, here goes," was Fitzgerald's reply, as at the head of his 300 Bengal Lancers he charged the Maratha cavalry.

Only for an instant did the Marathas resist this unexpected attack, and then they scattered in all directions, leaving behind them a small battery by which they had been supported. After pursuing them for a short distance Fitzgerald drew in his cavalry, and rode back to the Residency in triumph with the captured guns.

Filled with fresh courage by this splendid deed of daring, our troops on the hill, though exhausted by fifteen hours' fighting, charged down

THE BATTLE OF SITABALDI, FITZGERALD'S CHARGE

from the higher hill, and regained their lost position; and then with an almost superhuman effort the whole of our infantry, backed by the cavalry, charged down on the Marathas at the foot of the hill, capturing many of their guns and putting them to flight. By midday the fight was over, a fight which should ever be remembered with pride by all the sons of our Empire. How bloody it had been can be seen from the fact that a quarter of our total forces had been killed and wounded, including sixteen British officers.

All, however, was not yet over. Though badly beaten, Appa Sahib did not surrender; and collecting his scattered forces prepared for a fresh attack. Fortunately, however, for the British in Nagpur, the reinforcements which had been summoned, reached them during the next few days, and when Appa Sahib was again ready to attack, about a fortnight later, our position and numbers made us confident of the issue.

Hardly had the second battle of Nagpur begun, when word went out that Appa Sahib had actually surrendered. This, however, proved to be but a Maratha ruse, as when our troops advanced to take possession of his guns, a treacherous cannonade was at once opened on them. After severe fighting, in which rather heavy losses were incurred, the Maratha position was stormed, and the whole of their camp with forty elephants and sixty-three guns were taken.

Appa Sahib's career as a ruler did not, strange

to relate, at once come to an end. For various reasons he was given a further day of grace. Deprived of a large part of his territory including "the Saugor and Nerbudda Territories," he was allowed to continue the nominal ruler of South Gondwana under the eye of the British Resident. When, however, this leniency was made an excuse for still further intrigues with the Peshwa, and it was discovered that he was fomenting a rising amongst the Gonds, he was arrested and sent away to another part of India. On his way to his place of "retirement" he managed, however, to effect his escape in the uniform of a sepoy, whom he had bribed heavily, and after a good deal of further ineffectual scheming reached Rajputana, where he died some years after in comparative obscurity.

After Appa Sahib's final deposition, a grandson of Raghuji II, though still but a child, was recognised as Rajah, under the title of Raghuji III, and Baka Bai, a widow of Raghuji II, was appointed Regent. Her duties seemed to have been more those of a governess than a governor; as the affairs of the State were left entirely in the hands of Sir R. Jenkins, and a body of our officials appointed by him. Under his administration and that of his successor, the Honourable R. Cavendish, the country again became quiet and prosperous, trade increased, and the people were happy and contented.

Some years later when the young Rajah had

attained his majority, the administration of the country was again placed in Maratha hands, though still under the intimate supervision of the Resident. This condition of things lasted until the year 1853, when on the death of Raghuji III, without issue, the administration of the whole of the Bhonsla kingdom was taken over by the British Government.

So passed away the rule of the Marathas from Gondwana, and when it passed but a few regretted it. Its rulers had at their best been little more than soldiers of fortune. Few, if any, had been wise, or considerate of the welfare of their people. At times, through their selfishness, greed, and incompetency, the lot of the common people had been reduced to a state of abject misery and poverty. Life had been painfully insecure, and trade impossible. And when it became known that for the future the British were to administer the country, few were ready to oppose the new government. For the common people had already tasted something of the benefits of British rule, during the minority of their last Rajah, and knew by experience that under it they would find freedom, justice, and toleration.

CHAPTER X

A PLEA FOR THE OLD JOHN COMPANY

THERE are few achievements in human history of which a nation may be more justly proud, than the establishment of British rule in India. Little did our pleasure-loving monarch Charles II realise, as he signed the Charter of the East India Company more than two and a half centuries ago, that he was taking part in the first act of establishing an Empire in the East. Not that ideas of ruling India troubled the minds of the Company in those early days. Their vessels went off to the East on their long and weary voyages with one object alone—trade. Gradually, however, as trade grew, factories had to be established on the eastern and western coasts of India, and on the banks of some of her larger rivers; and with the establishment of these factories came the necessity of keeping order around them, and protecting them from attack.

Perilous days were those for the early settlers, with Maratha and Moslem often suspicious, sometimes actively hostile. But all the time the trade went on expanding, and the Company's sphere of influence went deeper and deeper into the heart of the Peninsula, until the East India Company found itself master of great tracts of country.

Then, though still but a company, it was faced by quite imperial tasks.

A Civil Service was needed to administer its territories, and an army to defend them; and Haileybury and Addiscombe in due time came into being, for the purpose of training men for their civil and military duties. The future rulers and generals of India, still mere boys, went forth to their life's work in the East, some of them to win reputations which will never die, some of them to find early graves.

It is indeed a strange story, the evolution of a trading company into an empire, and a great English historian has much to justify him in his rather quaint saying that "England stumbled into Empire."

Many hard and untrue things have been said of the old East India Company and its rule.

Doubtless there were Englishmen in India during its period who failed to uphold the high standard of British uprightness, justice, and mercy. With some of the most daring, as well as the most gifted, of her sons in the East, England was not always pleased; and while criticising, and even punishing them for their faults, strangely forgot the great services they had rendered.

But while we fully admit this, we must in all fairness add that there is no one page in the long history of England in which the names of so many great and noble characters can be found as in that which describes our English rule in India.

Where can one find names which speak more eloquently of Christian chivalry, of love of truth and righteousness, of hatred of oppression, of wisdom, firmness, and dauntless courage, than those of John and Henry Lawrence, Bartle Frere, Auckland Colvin, Montgomery, Herbert Edwardes, Donald McCleod, Outram, Havelock, John Nicholson, and Lord Roberts, all of them servants of this old East India Company ?

As to-day we contemplate the many evidences of our mild and beneficial rule in India, with peace and prosperity within its borders from the Himalayas to Cape Comorin, it is hard to realise what Old India was like, when our race first came into contact with it. Sir Mortimer Durand has given a description of it which for accuracy and breadth of view can hardly be excelled. He writes—

"When the East India Company entered upon its rise to Imperial domination, India, parcelled out among numerous chiefs, largely soldiers of fortune, had for generations been one vast war field, over which armies, aggregating perhaps 2,000,000 of men, many of them foreign free-lances, marched and fought, and ravaged. The sufferings of the people under such conditions need not be described. The Company rescued India from this state of chronic warfare and devastation, and gave to the Indian masses not only protection and peace, but the most beneficent rule they had ever known. Fitzjames Stephen, an English Judge, writing of the early days of the Company, has said that the whole Indian enterprise was 'not a tyrannical and detestable' one, but 'the greatest of English, one might almost say of human, enterprises.' There are no facts in history more clearly demonstrable than the facts that the Company rose to Imperial dominion with the goodwill and active help of vast numbers of Indians; and that when the Bengal army broke into revolt, as too powerful armies have done before, the Company's dominion was upheld, as it had been established, by the goodwill and active help of vast numbers of Indians. The districts which the revolt threw into anarchy, mainly districts in which the Bengal army was recruited, did not comprise a tenth part of India; not one of the great ruling chiefs joined the rebels; the smaller armies of Bombay and Madras remained faithful; and many thousands of Indians from the Bengal Presidency itself, enlisting of their own free will under the British Flag, fought with the British troops against the mutineers. Of the force which stormed Delhi not one-half, hardly more than a third, were white men. And so it was elsewhere. Then, as now, India was on our side, and the Mutiny was crushed. Since then the Crown has developed the work of the Company, ruling, as the Company rules, for the good of the people."

And, indeed, we may go further than Sir Mortimer Durand, and paint in even darker colours the moral and social misery of the people of those days. Sati[1] (the immolation of widows on the funeral pyre of their deceased husbands),

[1] See *Rambles and Recollections*, by Sir William Sleeman.

infanticide, human sacrifices to propitiate hostile gods and demons, self-inflicted tortures of various kinds, and frequent witch-murder, were widespread customs, rooted deeply in the minds of the people, and practised with the full approval of the conscience of the community.

Nor can it, I fear, be said that the spirit and convictions, which justified some of these cruel and unnatural practices, have entirely passed away. Not long ago, when visiting a remote State in Rajputana, I was taken to see the cenotaphs of the ancestors of its present Ruling Chief. The monuments were themselves richly carved and impressive. One of them stood over a place where fifty royal wives and mistresses had been burnt to death on the occasion of their lord's "burning"; and another marked the spot where eighty of these helpless women had perished under similar circumstances. It certainly seemed horribly cruel and revolting, and I expressed my feeling very plainly to my companion, the State Pandit, who was showing me round. Judge of my surprise at hearing his reply, uttered most courteously and quietly, "You English do not understand love."

Perhaps the best answer to those who speak ill of our rule in India is to bid them come and see it with their own eyes. Many distinguished travellers and statesmen from various European countries have done so in recent years, and the burden of their criticism has generally resembled that of

A PLEA FOR THE OLD JOHN COMPANY

Professor Garbe, a well-known German writer, who writes of the misfortunes that would befall India if to-day the beneficent and just rule of the English Government were to come to an end.

The first beginnings of British rule in Gondwana were not made till 1817, when, as we have seen, Appa Sahib, the Bhonsla ruler of Nagpur, as a punishment for his treachery, was deprived of the northern portion of his kingdom, that portion which corresponded roughly with the old Gond kingdom of Garha-Mandla.

Of the deplorable condition to which this territory was then reduced, we have a vivid picture from the pen of Sir Charles Grant, who at a later period of his service officiated as Chief Commissioner of the Central Provinces. Writing as he did, nearly two generations ago, with an intimate acquaintance of that part of Gondwana, we can the better realise what our just and tolerant administration has meant to the people in this part of India—

"This period (from 1798-1817), unfortunately for Jubbulpore, coincided with the worst period of Bhonsla administration. The Bhonsla government at this time had become arbitrary in its measures and corrupt in all its departments. All revenue reports of those times teem with accounts of the cruel, but often ingenious, processes by which Maratha collectors slowly bled the people. Villages were put up to the highest bidder, but even the purchaser was lucky if he got to the end of the year safe. After passing with alternating hope and fear the rainy season, and watching his crops safe through the caprices of the elements, some turn in the tide of war, or an unexpected robber-raid, might destroy all the fruits of the toil and expenditure of months. If the crops thus sown in sorrow, and tended in fear, came to maturity, there were fresh trials to encounter. Sometimes the lease taken at the beginning of the year, and carried through with so much difficulty and anxiety, was unceremoniously set aside in favour of a higher bidder, and the unfortunate lessee saw the harvest, on which he had staked his all, go to enrich some private enemy or clever speculator. Sometimes the village would be made over by the authorities to troops in arrears to pay themselves, no questions, of course, being asked. Sometimes the crop was seized directly by the government officials, without any pretence or form of reason. Taught by experience, the cultivators assumed the appearance of poverty, concealed their stock, and hung back from taking farms. But they were always worsted in the long run. Practically they had no choice except to cultivate, or to starve, and the assignee soon found out, by means of his spies, who were in the best position to take the leases. On these persons dresses and titles were liberally bestowed, and solemn engagements entered into, at a very moderate rate of rent, which engagements were most assuredly violated at the time of harvest, when the whole produce was at the mercy of the 'Jagirdar.' Thus the Maratha rulers proceeded from year to year, flattering the vanity of the 'malguzars' with dresses, titles, and other distinctions, and feeding their hopes with solemn promises, till all their capital was exhausted.

"There was a little more difficulty in tapping the wealth of bankers and others, whose substance was stored in a form less accessible and prominent than standing crops, or flocks and herds. Even in those times it was not for everyone to take the royal road, hit upon by Raghuji III, of going direct to the coveted strong boxes by means of burglary. So the notable device was discovered of *establishing 'adultery' courts, furnished with guards, fetters, stocks, and staff of witnesses.* When good information was obtained of the existence of a hoard of money, the unfortunate possessor was at once charged with adultery, and found guilty; and if the disgrace of a crime, which was held to reflect on the whole family of the accused, was not sufficient to bring him to reason, he was chained in the stocks till he agreed to pay ransom."

Perhaps when we read the following passage in this interesting report we shall the more fully realise the legacy of woe bequeathed by Marathas to the early British Administration—

"The Provisional Government appointed at Jubbulpore to carry on the administration of the newly-annexed Nerbudda country (1817) was called upon by its officials to decide among other questions whether '*widows should still be sold for the benefit of the State,*' whether one-fourth of the proceeds of all house sales should continue to be paid into the treasury, and whether '*persons selling their daughters*' should not still be taxed one-fourth of the price realised."

At a meeting of the same Provisional Government there is an entry ordering the release of a woman named Pursia, "who had been sold by auction a few days before *for seventeen rupees.*" "The taxes levied in different places varied with the idiosyncracies of the government, or of the individual tax-collector; but among them it may be noticed that people were mulcted for having houses to live in, or if they had no house, for their temporary sheds or huts; if they ate grain, their food was taxed at every stage in its progress through the country. If they ate meat, they paid duty on it through their butchers. When they married they paid for beating drums, or putting up marquees. If they rejoiced at the set Hindu festivals, they paid again; at the Holi, for instance, on the red powder which they threw at each other, at the Pola, on the ornaments which they tied to the horns of their cattle. In short, a poor man could not shelter himself, or clothe himself, or earn his bread, or eat it, or marry, or rejoice, or even ask his gods for better weather, without contributing separately on each individual act to the necessities of the State."

Nor were the sufferings of the unfortunate people confined to the ill-treatment of their Maratha rulers, for the whole of Northern

Gondwana was at that period overrun by wandering bands of robbers called "Pindaris," who, from their standing camps in Nerbudda valley, poured forth periodically carrying fire and sword. There is nothing in history more moving than the pictures of utter desolation which these human locusts left in their track.

Their plan of action is thus described by Malcolm—[1]

"The Pindaris were neither encumbered by tents, nor baggage; each horseman carried a few cakes of bread for his own subsistence, and some feeds of grain for his horse. The party, which usually consisted of two or three thousand good horses, with a proportion of mounted followers, advanced at the rapid rate of forty or fifty miles a day, neither turning to the right nor left till they arrived at their place of destination. They then divided and made a sweep of all the cattle and property they could find; committing at the same time the most horrid atrocities, and destroying what they could not carry away. They trusted to the secrecy and suddenness of the irruption for avoiding those who guarded the frontiers of the countries they invaded, and before a force could be brought against them they were on their return journey. Their chief strength lay in their being intangible. If pursued they made marches of extraordinary length, sometimes upwards of sixty miles, by roads almost impracticable for regular troops. If overtaken, they dispersed, and reassembled at an appointed rendezvous. Their

[1] *History of Central India.*

7—(3551)

wealth, their booty, and their families were scattered over a wide region, in which they found protection amid the mountains and in the fastnesses belonging to themselves and to those with whom they were either openly or secretly connected; but nowhere did they present any point of attack, and the defeat of a party, the destruction of one of their cantonments, or the temporary occupation of some of their strongholds, produced no effect beyond the ruin of an individual freebooter, whose place was instantly supplied by another, generally of more desperate fortune and therefore more eager for enterprise.

"But the ways of the Pindaris were not so very much worse than those of the more regularly-licensed plunderers, who called themselves revenue collectors. In Jubbulpore, in 1809, the maddened cultivators, exasperated by the exaction of a Maratha Subah, Narayan Roa, went so far as to call in the aid of the notorious Pindari leader, Amir Khan, preferring the crash of a sudden raid, with all its terrible accompaniments of fire and sword, to the slow torture of constant pressure, or perhaps hoping that in the general upset good men might chance to come uppermost. The landholders gained their object at first, as the arrival of the Pindari army so thoroughly frightened the Maratha governor that he quite forgot for the time to go on with his exactions; but before the plunderers left the country they had made themselves as much felt by their friends as by their foes, appropriating all they could seize, insulting the temples of the Hindus, defacing the images, and committing outrages and excesses such as will not be forgotten, or the horror excited by them be buried in oblivion."

And this story of woe has yet another page, which recalls the fact that the rapacity of the Maratha rulers, and the savage raids of the Pindaris, were not the only causes of the sorrows which were ever with the much afflicted people of North Gondwana in the early days of the last century.

No one can read Sir William Sleeman's chapter on "Thugs and Poisoners," in his *Rambles and Recollections*, and soon forget the horrors he there describes of that highly elaborated system of "religious" murder, which spread over large tracts of Northern and Central India at that time. To this distinguished soldier and administrator, who spent many years in these newly-acquired districts, we owe to a large extent the suppression of the Thugs, those fiends in human shape, who, after dedicating their weapons to the goddess Kali, and worshipping the setting sun, set off calmly to the execution of their murderous deeds.

"Between 1826 and 1835, 1,562 prisoners were tried by Sir William Sleeman at Jubbulpore for the crime of Thuggee, of whom 1,404 were hanged, or transported for life. Some individuals confessed to over 200, and one confessed to over 719 murders!"

CHAPTER XI

GONDWANA UNDER BRITISH RULE—EARLY DAYS

WHEN the Governor-General in Council had made his final decision to take over the administration of Northern Gondwana, it was not at first clear as to how the newly-acquired territories should be dealt with.

For a short time they were placed in the hands of a commissioner, who worked under the Resident at Nagpur.

Then, in the year 1820 they were formed into a "Division" with the title of "Saugor and Nerbudda Territories," and were placed in the charge of an agent, who worked directly under the Governor-General.

More than once during the succeeding years the "Saugor and Nerbudda Territories" were attached to the United Provinces (then called the North-West Provinces), only to pass back sooner or later into the hands of the Agent to the Governor-General at Jubbulpore.

Finally, on the death of Raghuji III, when Maratha rule passed away from the southern part of Gondwana, a new British Province was created under the title of "the Central Provinces," and the whole of Gondwana was placed in the hands of a Chief Commissioner.

GONDWANA UNDER BRITISH RULE

Twice during the years that lay between 1842 and 1859 our fellow-countrymen in Gondwana passed through anxious times. Early in 1842 their first trial came in what has since been called the Bundela rising. The rising was fortunately confined to the "Saugor and Nerbudda Territories," which border on those regions in Central India which are called Bundelkhand. The trouble arose, strange to relate, out of a sincere desire on our part to substitute improved civil courts of justice for the more primitive and imperfect system which had hitherto obtained in this part of the country. India is nothing if not conservative, and it is never easy to introduce anything new, even though it be a vast improvement on the old.

Very different to the comparatively insignificant Bundela rising of 1842 was the great Mutiny of 1857. Few, perhaps, spend any time to-day in reading of those stormy days, when the fate of our Indian Empire hung in the balance, and when but for the strong administrators and fearless soldiers of the old East India Company, "men who looked on tempests and whose hearts were never shaken," all traces of our rule in India might easily have been swept away.

The Mutiny was, curious to relate, hardly felt in Nagpur and in the southern portion of the Central Provinces. For this much credit is due to Mr. Ellis, the Deputy Commissioner of Nagpur, and to his brother officers.

Early in June it was known to them that secret meetings of a suspicious character were taking place every night in the native city, and that a general feeling of uneasiness was apparent in the Bazaar. Further enquiry made it clear that a number of troopers of the Bengal cavalry regiment, which then formed part of the garrison of Nagpur, were seriously disaffected.

Then came the startling intelligence that 13th June was the night planned by the mutineers for the rising, and that the ascent of a fire-balloon was to be the signal for its start. How the plot failed is an interesting story, which is worth the telling.

We now know that this cavalry regiment hoped to induce the Madras regiment of infantry and a battery of artillery, then at Nagpur, to come over to their side. They had made certain overtures to them, but things had not come to a head, when late in the afternoon of 13th June an unexpected order from the officer commanding the cavalry (acting in consultation with Mr. Ellis), viz., that one squadron was to hold itself immediately ready to march to Seoni, roused their suspicions.

The plans of mutineers, when disarranged, have a way of breaking down. Fancying that their plans might be upset, the sowars sent a native officer to the Madras infantry lines to endeavour to arouse them. This man, however, was quietly arrested before he reached the infantry

GATEWAY AT GOND PALACE, NAGPUR

lines, though the mutineers failed to discover it till too late.

Immediately after nightfall the Madras infantry and artillery were ordered by their officers to parade, and the way in which they obeyed orders, speedily removed any lingering doubts as to their loyalty. While they fell in, the guns of Sitabaldi Fort were trained on the cavalry lines, and the loyal garrison silently awaited the arrival of the mutineers.

Still unaware of what was happening, and although no fire balloon went up, the mutineers proceeded at ten o'clock to mount their horses for the attack. Judge of their surprise when, as they rode forward, they found themselves face to face with the loyal infantry and artillery, and learnt that the guns of Sitabaldi Fort were ready to mow them down at the word of command.

Realising that resistance was useless, they surrendered, dismounted, and gave up their arms. After a careful enquiry, five of their ringleaders, native officers, and two leading Mohammedan merchants in the city, were put on their trial, found guilty, and hanged from the ramparts of the fort.

It is interesting to know, that during this whole crisis, the aged Maratha princess, Baka Bai Bhonsla, remained absolutely loyal, and exercised considerable influence on our behalf in the Maratha districts. Had an important Maratha

State, such as Nagpur, so soon after its annexation, broken out into revolt, the effect on South India generally would have been most serious.

In Jubbulpore and the northern part of the Central Provinces the mutiny came to a head more slowly, and in the long run proved far more troublesome. Weeks before its actual outbreak, it was evident to the Commissioner, Colonel Erskine (afterwards Earl of Mar and Kellie), that serious trouble was brewing. To the suggestion that it might be wiser to send all the English ladies away to a place of safety, and to withdraw himself with the other British officials to Nagpur, he gave an emphatic refusal. The Residency was put in a state of defence (for a time it was popularly known as "Fort Erskine"), and all the English residents moved either inside its walls, or within its "compound." During this period of suspense, we read, amongst other things, that the Sunday church services were held in the Residency, though the chaplain, from time to time, felt it his duty to conduct services in the station church, when his congregations were, as might have been expected, not overwhelmingly large!

For a time, indeed, it seemed as if the impending storm would be averted. Then, however, came the discovery of a plot on the part of the pensioner, Gond Rajah, and his son, inciting the native infantry regiment to rise, and massacre all the English residents. After due trial, both father

GATEWAY AT GOND PALACE, NAGPUR

and son were found guilty, and on the night after their execution, the regiment mutinied and marched out of Jubbulpore, without its British officers, with the avowed intention of joining the mutineers at Delhi.

Their departure was the commencement of a period of anarchy and confusion in all the country which lay to the north of Jubbulpore. More than one severe action, and many minor ones, were fought, and more than one British officer fell when leading his men, often against heavy odds. Amongst those who lost their lives in those troublous times, was Major Jenkins, the Assistant Quarter-Master General of the Jubbulpore force, uncle of the last Chief Justice of Calcutta. His grave may still be seen in the old cemetery at Jubbulpore. Not until early in 1858, when General Sir Hugh Rose marched through Bundelkhand, and defeated the rebels in several engagements, was the back of the Mutiny really broken in North Gondwana. Early in May, 1858, an amnesty was proclaimed, and on 1st August Colonel Erskine was able to announce that the Mutiny was at an end.

CHAPTER XII

GONDWANA UNDER BRITISH RULE

IT certainly requires some effort of imagination, as one moves about Gondwana to-day, to picture what the unhappy Gondwana of Maratha days must have resembled. For much has been accomplished in the two generations which have passed since the Government of India, realising the isolated position of Gondwana, and the futility of connecting it with their older Provinces, made their wise decision and created the new British Province, henceforth to be called the Central Provinces, under the control of a Chief Commissioner.

Not a little of this rapid development is unquestionably due to the ability of the men who have held that office. As one looks down the roll of Chief Commissioners who have administered the Central Provinces for longer or shorter periods since 1861, one sees the names of some who have gained lasting reputations in Indian administration. More than one of the most brilliant, however, held this high office in the Central Provinces for too short a period to accomplish all they wished to do, and won their reputations in other fields.

Of those who have left a permanent mark on the Central Provinces, the name of the late Mr.

Richard Temple, afterwards Sir Richard Temple, the second on the roll of Chief Commissioners, must always stand out pre-eminent. Before our present excellent system of railways, and long before the days of motors, he traversed thousands of miles, generally on horseback, and over trackless jungles, to see things with his own eyes. Few of the needs of his great charge seem to have escaped his notice. Possessed of energy, which even the climate of India did not sensibly diminish, he accomplished great things during his nearly five years of office.

During the earlier period of his administration he organised two large exhibitions of art and industry at Nagpur and Jubbulpore, for the purpose of educating and stimulating the industrial and agricultural life of the people. His description of these exhibitions recalls vividly the second Nagpur Exhibition, inaugurated nearly fifty years later by his successor Mr. Reginald Craddock.

"To these great displays the natives of all classes, high and humble, flocked in tens of thousands. Before their wondering gaze were shown not only the products from distant parts of their own country, but also specimens of the manufactures of Western lands. The ornamental work from Europe would, it was fondly, perhaps vainly, supposed, inform their minds with fresh ideas of the beautiful, while the machinery and implements might give them an impression of powers and forces unknown before, and so fill them with reflection regarding the useful. The objects which we thus set before ourselves were but imperfectly realised. The exhibitions were wonders for a time only, though it may be hoped that some educational result was produced by all the labour which we bestowed on their preparation. One effect at least they had, namely this, that the Civil officers and the merchants gained a far more accurate knowledge than they would otherwise have possessed, regarding the resources and manufactures of these remote provinces, and thus some stimulus was given to trade."

One of the early questions which seems to have engaged Sir Richard Temple's attention was the overhauling and improvement of the land revenue system and the rights of tenants. Under the Maratha *régime* a system of petty landlordism had spread over the country, and tenants were liable to ejectment at any moment, simply at the caprice of their landlord. The beginnings of our present system, whereby a tenant has certain recognised rights over the land, as long as he pays his rent, were introduced by Sir Richard Temple, and have been carried still further forward by succeeding Chief Commissioners.

We have already alluded to the attention which the old Gond rulers of Gondwana paid to the important question of irrigation, and to quote from Sir Richard Temple, "how they stopped up the gorges by dams of massive masonry, the valleys then filling with water, and becoming

FALLS OF THE NERBUDDA, NEAR JUBBULPORE

reservoirs, some five, some even twenty miles in circumference, worthy to be called artificial lakes." When we call to mind the fact that certainly 96 per cent. of the people of India live on the soil, and depend for the watering of their fields on the annual "monsoon" rains, which are always uncertain, and sometimes fail them altogether, we can the better realise the supreme importance of conserving and distributing water over as wide an area as possible. By no one was the importance of irrigation more thoroughly recognised than by Sir Richard Temple, and it is interesting to reflect that the small beginnings of his day have been carried on unceasingly ever since, so that at the present time considerable portions of the Central Provinces have ceased to be entirely dependent on a single year's rainfall.

One piece of political foresight on the part of Sir Richard Temple, which has borne excellent fruit in Gondwana, is worthy of mention. A limited number of the leading Gond landlords in Southern Gondwana, were raised to the position of Feudatory Chiefs, or petty Rajahs. Later on a Chief's College was opened for the education of their sons at Raipur, and the happy contrast between what we see of the younger chiefs, and what we hear of their ancestors, justifies us in hoping for steady improvement in these small Gond States.

Nor was Sir R. Temple forgetful, in spite of the

pressing needs of the great native population around him, of the interests of his own race, especially those of the poor Anglo-Indians, the "domiciled community" as they are now called. In his time, and with his help and sympathy, the Bishop Cotton school was opened at Nagpur, for boys and girls of this class, followed some years later by the Christ Church schools at Jubbulpore. The former school was opened shortly after Bishop Cotton's visit to Nagpur, and was called after him. He, in his earlier days, had been head master of Marlborough College, and during his ten years' Indian episcopate did much for the education of the Eurasian class in India.

Nor can our Church in the Central Provinces quite forget what she owes to Sir Richard Temple. Convinced of the truth of Christianity, and recognising the importance of Christian conduct and example in the lives of the ruling race, he made an enquiry into the spiritual condition of the scattered European and Eurasian communities in the new Province. Backed by his help and sympathy, small churches were built in many of our small civil stations, partly by private effort, and partly by Government grant-in-aid, which have since been a source of comfort to many. During his time the parish church of Nagpur, which has recently been transformed by the late Mr. G. F. Bodley into All Saints' Cathedral, was completed. It is interesting to note that Bishop Cotton himself visited Nagpur for its Consecration,

KEATING POINT, PACHMARHI

and that the petition for its Consecration was read by Sir Richard Temple.

During Sir Richard Temple's period of administration, and under his direction, diligent search was made in the Satpura Hill country for a suitable hill-station for the Central Provinces. The honour of discovering Pachmarhi, which was the hill-station eventually selected, belongs to Captain Forsyth. It is interesting, however, to note that one of those to whom the special duty of clearing the plateau of Pachmarhi of its undergrowth was entrusted, still lives on at an advanced age in Jubbulpore, the Rev. P. Cullen, M.D. In those days, as Civil Surgeon of Khandwa, Dr. Cullen was a well-known figure in the Central Provinces. In later years, after retiring as Surgeon-Colonel of the Indian Medical Service, he was ordained by the Bishop of Calcutta to assist in the work at Jubbulpore.

It must be remembered that Nagpur, the headquarters of the administration, lies in the plains country to the south of the Satpura plateau, and has a rather unenviable notoriety for high temperatures in the hot weather. After a careful examination of various places, the beautiful little park-like plateau of Pachmarhi was eventually selected, a charming spot about 3,500 feet above sea-level, surrounded by hills, several of which are nearly 1,000 feet higher than the plateau itself. For many years past this has been the summer resort for Europeans in the Central Provinces;

and its giant canyons, descending in some cases to a quite extraordinary depth into the bowels of the mountains, as well as the magnificent cliffs of its surrounding mountains, make its scenery quite unique.

It is not easy for the modern resident in the Central Provinces, who regards a journey to Bombay or Calcutta as a matter of no consequence, to realise that neither Jubbulpore nor Nagpur was connected by rail with either of these great Indian cities in the early days of the Central Provinces Administration. Not until 20th February, 1867, was Nagpur connected with Bombay, and not until 8th March, 1870, was the line from Calcutta to Bombay, which passes through Jubbulpore, first opened.

At the banquet given by the Great Indian Peninsula Company at Jubbulpore, when H.R.H. the Duke of Edinburgh, and the Earl of Mayo—then Viceroy—were present, the latter, in proposing the toast " Success and Prosperity " to the G.I.P. Railway, made the following remarks—

" On this day the great distance of 1,070 miles of the Great Indian Peninsula Railway system has been opened to the public ; Calcutta and Bombay are brought into close connection, and this great Peninsula is at last bridged by a railway 1,300 miles in length. When we look back to the history of this undertaking we must recollect the very great difficulties which attended its early progress. The thing is now comparatively easy,

WATERS MEET, PACHMARHI

much more is known, the organisation of labour is less difficult, and our able engineers have the light of experience and history to guide them. But in the early days of this undertaking far greater difficulties which no longer exist had to be encountered, and therefore we must make due allowance for what may perhaps seem a rather protracted period over which these works have extended. During that time periods of great scarcity occurred; the Mutiny also occurred in the early history of this enterprise, and there have been several violent outbreaks of disease, and when we look back upon the whole history of this railway we may well wonder at the perseverance by which, in its earlier stages, the work was carried on."

Great were the rejoicings, so Sir Richard Temple tells us in his Memoirs, in Nagpur and Jubbulpore, at these important events, "as the local residents rejoiced at being able to fly away for recreation or in quest of health when sick, the engineers were light-hearted at the remembrance of anxieties dissipated and toils ended, and the Administration exhilarated by the thought of material resources augmented and opportunities enlarged."

After these important events in the railway world an additional scheme was contemplated for a line which should run from Nagpur eastwards, and "tap the surplus produce of the Chhattisgarh region, which was over-stocked with grain." Old residents in Nagpur still recall the days when the

Chhattisgarh State railway ran its metre-gauge line from Nagpur to Rajnandgaon. Later on, largely through the indomitable energy of Mr. T. Wynne, the Bengal-Nagpur Railway Company, making Nagpur their headquarters, acquired this line, transforming it into the broad-gauge system, and linking it up with the East India Railway Company at Asansol. Of the further developments of that progressive railway company, of their new route into Calcutta *via* Khargpur, and of their widespread system of light railways in Gondwana, we need not speak. The beginnings of these things belong but to yesterday.

If we have spoken at considerable length of Sir Richard Temple's work in the Central Provinces, it is because it fell to his lot to be the pioneer British Administrator of Gondwana.

While it is impossible to speak as freely of those who are still with us, as of those " who rest from their labours," and while most of Sir Richard Temple's successors have added something of greater or lesser importance to the foundations which he laid nearly two generations ago, some reference may fairly be made to what the Central Provinces owes to its last Chief Commissioner, Sir Reginald Craddock.

Previous to his appointment the Province had suffered seriously from the fact that not a few of its Chief Commissioners had but little personal knowledge of this part of India, and had hardly entered on their new office when they were called away to some higher appointment in the Government of India.

With an intimate knowledge of the needs of the Province in which he had spent the whole of his service, Sir Reginald Craddock entered on his work as Chief Commissioner, and for five years administered the Province with marked ability. During this period a second Nagpur industrial exhibition was held, about fifty years after the exhibition organised by Sir Richard Temple. If it was followed, as is generally admitted, with more encouraging results, it was doubtless because the country was more ready for it.

Concentrating a good deal of attention on Nagpur, which had been, hitherto, the least attractive headquarters' station in India, Sir Reginald Craddock practically created the new and handsome civil station. Nor was he forgetful of the large native city of Nagpur, with its population of 130,000 souls. "Ill-built and uninteresting," was the only description which Sir Richard Temple could give of it, and he might well have added, extremely unhealthy. Under Sir Reginald Craddock's vigorous administration a further water-supply was provided, and the beginning of a sound system of city drainage was introduced. Old houses were pulled down, and new streets built, or planned. A new residential suburb for Indian gentry was created (now called Craddock Town), and last, but not least, the foundations were laid of an excellent Market Hall in cleanly surroundings.

Nor has the forward movement in Nagpur, which he inaugurated, in any sense weakened in the hands of his successor. Already Nagpur is preparing itself for a fine residential University, in which the Hislop Missionary College and the Morris College—a Government college named after Sir John Morris, a former Chief Commissioner—will form constituent parts; and a Medical School for the training of assistant doctors for the needs of the Central Provinces has recently been opened.

A distinguished Norwegian writer, Professor Sten Konow, has written some interesting lines on the industrial development of India under British rule. "It cannot be denied," he writes, "that the English in India have accomplished a great deal. The administration of the country is excellent. The economic life of the country has progressed so surprisingly that India now plays a very important *rôle* in the world traffic."

While the cotton mills of Bombay and Cawnpore, "the Manchester of India," and the jute-mills of Bengal, are conspicuous features on the landscapes of these parts of India, it is not perhaps generally known that old Gondwana is already playing an ever-increasing part in the industrial life of the country. Ever since the American Civil War caused an extraordinary demand for

A PORTION OF THE OLD GOND FORT, NAGPUR

Indian cotton, the regions south of the Satpuras, in Berar and Nagpur, have been exporting enormous quantities of cotton to Japan and Europe. Probably there is no great stretch of country in all India which excels the black-cotton country of Berar in fertility. It is also interesting to note that while a good deal of the raw product, after passing through the ginning factories which are to be seen dotted all over that part of the country, is transported to other lands, much of it is being used in the manufacture of cotton goods in India itself. There is no sight in Nagpur more full of human interest than the Empress Cotton Mills, which employ over 7,000 Indian hands, and are under the entire control of an enterprising firm of Parsees.

To one who, like the writer, has spent some years of his life amid the collieries and blast furnaces of Durham, there is always a peculiar interest in visiting the collieries and manganese mines of the Central Provinces. At Umaria, at picturesque Mohpani, at the Pench valley collieries, or at Ballarshah, in the Chanda District, one seems to be back again in the busy North of England. Nor are there any visits in my frequent journeyings to which I look forward more heartily than those which take me to the manganese mines of Bhandara, where, from time to time, in some mining engineer's bungalow, I am asked to hold Divine Service for those who are engaged in this important branch of industrial work.

Our aim has been but to give a general impression of the progress and development of old Gondwana under British rule, and more than this we may not attempt. Gondwana has its own special needs, which are constantly before the minds of those who are responsible for its administration. If it is in some ways the most contented region in India, it preserves this Eden-like condition very probably because the majority of its people are still uneducated. How to enlighten its people and to keep them at the same time contented is a problem which the future has to solve. That there is a real need for improved agricultural methods is obvious, and much is being done by our Government Agricultural Department, not only in its admirable Agricultural College at Nagpur and on its few experimental farms, where various seeds and "crossings" are tested, but also by a widely-spread system of small "demonstration" farms, or holdings, dotted over various districts, where the villagers can see for themselves what superior ploughing and manuring with good seeds can produce in the way of crops. And yet, in spite of all this excellent work of government, it is obvious to those who really know the Indian ryot that extraordinary patience and tact are needed to overcome his besetting sins of foolish conservatism and lethargy. Gondwana, too, like other parts of India, is beginning to develop its industrial life. How to attract a fair proportion of its educated youths away from the fascinations of the Law Courts into the pursuits of an industrial life is a goal towards which our education may well aim.

And last, but assuredly not least, how to bring some kind of simple and useful education to the great masses of the village people, who are still quite illiterate, is another portion of the White Man's burden. Already amongst other such things a useful School of Handicrafts has been started by the Government in Nagpur for the purpose of teaching village boys the use of improved tools, and better and more modern methods of working. Forty youths, mostly the sons of village carpenters and blacksmiths, are at present passing through this course of instruction, and will return in due time to start life in their own villages, far better equipped than their fathers were before them.

What we must hope is that the beginnings of better things which have been made in this and other parts of India, may be given time to grow and mature; and that taught by the failures of the past, we may be wiser in the future in understanding the exact needs of our great Eastern Dependency.

CHAPTER XIII

SOME STRANGE BELIEFS AND CUSTOMS IN GONDWANA

INDIA is certainly the home of strange beliefs and customs, and nowhere are they found more abundantly than among her aborigines. Hidden away in remote jungles or in hilly tracts, these people live their lives in ignorance of the forward march of civilisation and still cling to many of their old superstitions.

One influence has alone seriously affected the aborigines of Gondwana during the course of the centuries, and that clearly comes from the Hindus who dwell amongst them. On the other hand, it can hardly be doubted but that some of the least worthy elements in Hinduism have come into it from purely aboriginal sources.

It is to be remembered that the aborigines of India number many millions, perhaps twenty, and amongst them are found marked varieties of race and culture. The almost naked Nagas, the Abors and Mishmis, who live in the hills which border on the Assam valley, and who are Mongols in origin, are in most respects no more advanced than some of the wildest races in Central Africa. They still practise head-hunting, whenever the opportunity presents itself.

The Gond, however, has for long centuries put

MANDHATA ISLAND ON THE NERBUDDA

away such savagery, and is, as a rule, a mild and gentle creature. Really brave, when following wild game in his own jungles, he is in the presence of strangers reserved and timid; and it is only after considerable acquaintance and much questioning that one can discover what his real beliefs are.

To begin with his theology. One curious feature of a Gond's theology is to be found in the number of gods he recognises. It might be thought that such a question as the exact number of gods a person worships belongs merely to the reign of speculation, and can have but little effect on practical life; but this is by no means the case with the Gond. On the number of gods he worships depends the special group or family to which he belongs; and connected with this are the families into which he may marry. Worshippers of seven gods may not marry into their own group, but must select partners from among the six-god, five-god, or four-god families. The Raj-Gonds, whose ancestors either held land under the old Gond kings, or were a sub-tribe connected with the ruling families, are all six-god worshippers. A Raj-Gond servant of mine tells me that to marry in his own group would be the same as marrying his own sister.

Hislop, the well-known Scottish missionary, thought he had found traces of no less than fifteen gods amongst them—but later research tends to show that there are no more than seven in their Pantheon.

The Gonds recognise one of these seven gods, Bhera Pen, sometimes called Maha-Deva, as the creator of the world. He has no symbol or idol, but iron is sacred to him. As, however, he is a kindly being, who takes almost no interest in his creatures, he is seldom worshipped. The gods that the Gond has to reckon with, are those malignant spirits which are always on the look out to take offence and do him harm. These cruel, and often nameless spirits, who are ever ready to lay in wait for a man and bring evil upon him, must be propitiated at all cost.

From this it is obvious that the main religious acts of the Gonds are inspired by fear. They are like children, who can count on no kind of help from their father, who, though not ill-natured, is unable or unwilling to assist them. Their one concern is to keep on good terms with their known and unknown spiritual enemies.

Canon Wood mentions, however, a religious ceremony amongst the Gonds of the Chanda District, which seems to him to " embody a dim idea of a protecting god." " The tutelary deity of the six-god Gonds is symbolised by six spear-heads, one large and five small spear-heads, of the five-god Gonds by one large and four small spear-heads, and so on for the others. When the Gond desires the protection of his ' House ' god, these are taken down from the tree where they are hung in a skin bag, are daubed with red paint

CHAMBER OF HORRORS, DEOGARH

or blood, and goats, fowls, rice, and 'daru,'[1] are sacrificed to them, the ceremony ending, like all Gond ceremonies, with feasting, drinking, and a dance."

In olden days human sacrifices were common in Gondwana, until put down by the firm hand of the British rule. At Deogarh, the capital of the Eastern Middle Kingdom, one is still shown "the chamber of horrors" where human sacrifices were offered by the king before going on an expedition. As late as 1842, when the Rajah of Bastar went on a long journey, twenty-five human victims were sacrificed at Dantewara temple to secure for him an undisturbed journey.

Two places in old Gondwana were specially famous for a peculiar form of human sacrifice, which, for lack of a better word, may be described as "religious suicide."

One of these places was a cliff on the side of the hill of Mahadeva, not far from the entrance to its well-known cave, and only two or three miles from Pachmarhi; the other, called the Birkhila, or hero's step, was a cliff on the Island of Mandhata, overlooking the Nerbudda, and not far from the Onkar temple of Shiva. Both places, be it observed, were closely connected with the worship of Shiva "the Destroyer."

The persons who made this horrible sacrifice were, so Malcolm[2] tells us, generally of low caste,

[1] Country liquor distilled from the Mahua tree.

[2] Malcolm's *Memoirs of Central India,* Vol. II, p. 210.

and one of the leading motives by which they were actuated was the belief that they would be reborn as Rajahs in the next state of transmigration. In many cases they were the first-born sons of women who had long been barren, and who, to remove what they deemed a curse, had vowed their child (if one was given them) to Onkar (Shiva) of Mandhata.

Forsyth[1] gives us such a vivid picture of one such sacrifice witnessed by an unnamed English officer in 1824, and written by him in the Nimar records, that I feel compelled to give it, terrible though it was, in his exact words. The Island of Mandhata at that time was not in British territory, and so force could not be used to prevent this gruesome sacrifice.

The writer, however, seems to have done all he could to dissuade the unfortunate creature from destroying himself, but unfortunately failed in his efforts.

"I took care to be present at an early hour at the representation of Bhairon,[2] a rough block of basalt smeared with red paint, before which he must necessarily present and prostrate himself, ere he mounted to the lofty pinnacle whence to spring on the idol. Ere long he arrived, preceded by rude music. He approached the amorphous idol with a light foot, while a wild pleasure marked

[1] Capt. Forsyth's *Highlands of Central India*, p. 181.

[2] Bhairon and his spouse the goddess Kali are believed by the ignorant to feed on human flesh.

ONKAR TEMPLE AND BIRKHILA CLIFF, MANDHATA

his countenance. As soon as this subsided, and repeatedly during the painful scene, I addressed myself to him, in the most urgent possible manner, to recede from his rash resolve, pledging myself to ensure him protection and a competence for his life. I had taken the precaution to have a boat close at hand, which in five minutes would have transported us beyond the sight of the multitude. In vain I urged him. He now more resolutely replied that it was beyond human power to remove the sacrifice of the powerful Bhairon. So deep-rooted a delusion could only be surmounted by force; and to exercise that I was unauthorised. While confronted with the idol, his delusion gained strength; and the barbarous throng cheered with voice and hand, when by his motions he indicated a total and continued disregard of my persuasions to desist. He made his offering of cocoanuts, first breaking one; and he emptied into a gourd presented by the priestess his previous collection of pice and cowries. She now tendered to him some ardent spirit in the nutshell, first making her son drink some from his hand, to obviate all suspicion of its being drugged. A little was poured in libation on the idol. She hinted to him to deliver to her the silver rings he wore. In doing so he gave a proof of singular collectedness. One of the first he took off he concealed in his mouth till he had presented to her all the rest, when, searching among the surrounding countenances, he pointed to a man to whom he ordered this ring to be given. It was a person who had accompanied him from Ujjain. An eagerness was now evinced by several to submit bracelets, and even betel-nuts, to his sacred touch. He composedly placed such in his mouth and returned them. The priestess at last presented him with a pan leaf, and he left the spot with a firm step, amidst the plaudit of the crowd. During the latter half of his ascent he was much concealed from view by shrubs. At length he appeared to the aching sight, and stood in a bold and erect posture upon the fatal eminence. Some short time he passed in agitated motions on the stone ledge, tossing now and then his arms aloft as if employed in invocation. At length he ceased; and, in slow motions with both his hands, made farewell salutations to the assembled multitude. This done, he whirled down the cocoanut, mirror, knife, and lime, which he had continued to hold; and stepping back was lost to view for a moment. The next second he burst upon our agonised sight in a most manful leap, descending feet foremost with terrific rapidity, till, in mid career, a projecting rock reversed his position, and caused a headlong fall. Instant death followed this descent of ninety feet, and terminated the existence of this youth, whose strength of faith and fortitude would have adorned the noblest cause."

Some years ago a friend of mine who was then administering the Bastar State, was called upon to try an old Gond for sacrificial murder. The following facts emerged in the course of the trial. A dam had been built by the Gonds in a certain neighbourhood to hold up the water which fell during the rainy season. It was a matter of great importance that this dam should stand firm, as it affected the comfort and even the lives of many. For two or three years, just as the tank was at its fullest, this dam always gave way at a certain place, and all the labour bestowed on it was thrown away. Then it was darkly hinted that an evil spirit was the cause of all their trouble, and that he could be propitiated by nothing less than a human sacrifice.

Possessed of the idea that by this means alone could the dam be made to stand, the old Gond brooded for weeks. Then as he sat one day by the empty tank, an old hag, of over threescore years and ten, and in her dotage, staggered passed him. Surely the gods had sent him a victim, to whom life was no longer precious! . . . And so the deed was done, the sacrifice offered, and to add to the pathos of it all, the dam stood firm where the old woman's corpse lay hid.

My friend had no option but to sentence the murderer to death, but he did so with deep regret. The Gond met his death quite bravely, convinced that he had rendered a real service to his village.

A strange ceremony still takes place every year at Jagadalpur, the capital of Bastar State, during the Hindu Festival of Dasehra. The principal shrine in this wild country is a temple dedicated to the goddess Dantesvari, once known as Rakhta Danti, "the bloody-toothed,"[1] another name for the fierce goddess Kali. This goddess was, so the people of Bastar believe, the household goddess of the family of their present ruling chief,

[1] *Epigraphia Indica,* No. 30. Dantewara inscriptions by Rai Bahadur Hira Lal, B.A.

when his Rajput ancestors ruled in Hastinapura and Warangal. When driven from the latter place by the Mohammedan invasion he fled into Bastar, and in response to his entreaties, this goddess promised to follow him, ordering him to advance as long as he heard "the tinkling of her anklets" behind him, and promising if he did so he would overcome all his enemies.

As they crossed the confluence of the Sankini and Dankini rivers, the feet of the goddess sank deep in the sand, and hearing no sound the Rajah turned round. On this the goddess became angry and reproached him with his want of faith. After a time, however, she relented, and told him that he might proceed with the conquest of the country, but she, for her part, would remain where she was. At this spot her famous shrine now stands, at which, till comparatively recently, human sacrifices were offered.

"Nothing is done," so Colonel Glasfurd writes of Bastar in 1862, "no business undertaken, without consulting her; not even will the Rajah or Diwan proceed on a pleasure party or hunting expedition without consulting 'Mai' (mother). Her advice is asked in matters of the most trivial nature; flowers are placed on the head of the idol, and as they fall to the right or to the left, so is the reply interpreted as favourable or otherwise."

Once a year at the Festival of Dasehra the Ruling Chief of Bastar divests himself of all clothing, save a loin cloth dyed to resemble his

THE RAJAH OF BASTAR IN HIS TRIUMPHAL CAR

own skin, and with a garland of flowers on his head, mounts a large wooden car, not altogether unlike the Jagannath Car at Puri. In this car, surrounded by some of the leading men of his capital, he is drawn through the streets of Jagadalpur, while his subjects, principally Gonds, fall prostrate before him. He is regarded for the time being, so it is said, as a kind of incarnation of a god, a "Hinduized version of the ancient Gond god Pharsa Pen," the spouse of the goddess Dantesvari. On such occasions in former days human beings threw themselves under the car as sacrifices, and even now young buffaloes and goats are frequently pushed under it.

Witchcraft is still very prevalent in Gondwana, and is often responsible for much cruelty and occasionally even for murders.

One such murder was described to me quite recently by the Deputy Commissioner of a district in which I was touring. A Gond village had been visited by severe sickness, men, women, and children had sickened and some had died; there had been heavy mortality amongst the cattle. At length the village elders met, and after some discussion decided that there was a witch in the village. After examining all the women, an old woman was selected as being the cause of all the trouble. No one was ready to defend her, and she was seized, buried in the ground up to her arm-pits, and mercilessly beaten till she died.

Canon Wood mentions a curious custom amongst

the Gonds in his district, which recalls the Western custom of "ducking the witch." If a woman is suspected of being a witch, she is thrown into the nearest tank or pond. If she remains under the water, while a man shoots three arrows into the air, she is innocent, but if she comes to the surface before that she is proved to be a witch. Her two front teeth are then knocked out, her head shaved, and she is banished from the village.

Sometimes, as one passes from one Gond village to another, one's attention is called to a quaint little cart, hardly larger than a child's toy, which lies at the side of a jungle track. There it lies full of rubbishy offerings, and there it has been brought by the people of some village in a time of epidemic. Along with it the villagers trusted they were bringing the cruel demon who had been tormenting them. All that they asked of him, as they left him in his solitude, was that he would stay there, or even go to another village, but never return to them.

In his little book on *The Story of the Gond Mission,* the Rev. J. Fryer mentions certain curious superstitions, connected with trees, amongst the Gonds in his district. These superstitions are based on the widespread conviction amongst many of these simpler races, who are still in the animistic stage, that, "whenever savages see motion, they imagine a spirit." A common belief exists "that some trees must not be struck at night, for fear that the sleep of the tree spirit may be disturbed ; that, before climbing a tree one should pray for its pardon for the rough usage it is about to be subjected to ; that, if a mango tree withers, and then grows again, the tree spirit was absent on pilgrimage."

One curious Gond custom seen all over Gondwana in its wildest regions is the setting up of a clay image of a tiger to mark the place where a man has been slain by one of these wild animals. The idea is that the image of the tiger called "Waghoba" is indwelt by the soul of the dead man, who, in hatred of his slayer, will act as a village guardian.

The belief in "totems" is everywhere found amongst the Gonds, and many are the plants and animals which are regarded as "sacred." The late Major Lucie Smith, a well-known authority in South Gondwana, stated that each of the four well-known groups of Gonds had their own special "totem"—the four-god Gonds regarding the tortoise and crocodile as their totem; the five-god Gonds the iguana ; the six-god Gonds, the tiger ; and the seven-god Gonds, the porcupine.

The position of women amongst the Gonds, as, indeed, amongst all the aborigines of India, is largely one of equality with the opposite sex, and where Hindu ideas have not penetrated, the woman is free to marry the man of her choice. Few marriages take place before the girl is full grown.

Amongst the Maria Gonds of the Chanda district there is a "bachelors" quarter in every village, where the young men are shut up at night!

After a couple of Maria Gonds have been keeping company for a little, the village elders and parents step in, and the betrothal is arranged. Shortly after this the bridegroom's party come and plant a spear in the court-yard of the bride's house. If the bride's party consent, water is poured over the spear by the girl's father. Should he fail to do this, it is regarded as a grievous insult, and he is fined heavily.

The marriage ceremony is simplicity itself. A platform of cow-dung cakes is built, on which a blanket is spread. On this the young couple stand and exchange vows. The bridegroom puts an iron ring on one of the bride's fingers, and the ceremony is over. The newly married couple spend their short honeymoon in a temporary hut previously prepared in the forest.

In certain cases where the bridegroom is too poor to pay the price which is demanded by the father for his daughter, he is allowed to serve, like the Patriarch Jacob, for his wife. This service sometimes lasts for several years.

Unlike the higher castes of Hindus the Gonds raise no objection to the marriage of widows. Such marriages are attended with a curious practice in one part of Gondwana. The couple stand under the eaves of the bridegroom's hut with an upright spear between them. Turmeric mixed with oil is poured over the bridegroom's head, and on the spear-head, and the bridegroom ties a string of beads around the bride's neck. After this simple ceremony he conducts her as his wife into his hut.

In some cases the Gonds bury their dead, and in some cases, where Hindu influence is strong, they burn them. The burial ground or burning place is generally to the east of the village. Their dead are sometimes buried with their feet towards the north; the explanation of this practice being a tradition that their home was once in the north.

The belief in transmigration is now growing amongst the Gonds in many places. One custom in connection with it is decidedly interesting. When a Gond is dying he is removed from his simple cord-bed and laid on the ground. Under his head is placed a small heap of grain. After his death, when the body is removed, an inverted basket is placed over this heap of grain. On the following day the village elders examine it, and the wise amongst them believe that they can detect the footprints of the animal into which the soul of the deceased has entered.

Canon Wood mentions a practice in connection with the dead which is worthy of a place in our record of some of the strange customs of Gondwana.

When the body of the dead has been carried to its last resting-place, the mourners, still bearing the corpse on their shoulders, face west. In front of them, ten paces away, are placed three "yen" leaves in a little line, about a yard apart. The first leaf is for the supreme god, the second for disembodied spirits, and the third for witches. The spirit of the departed is then called upon to disclose the cause of his death. The bearers, impelled by the spirit of the dead man, move forward to the leaves. If they stop at the first leaf, the dead man was recalled by the supreme spirit, and died a natural death. If they stop at the second leaf, he was slain by a malign spirit. If they stop at the third leaf, the cause of his death was witchcraft. In this case the spirit of the dead is invoked to reveal the sorcerer, who, if in the crowd, is at once seized and put on his or her trial.

It is a strange and pathetic fact that spirits of the dead are generally regarded more as objects of fear than as objects of love and veneration. Especially are those dreaded who have died violent or unnatural deaths. The spirit of the woman who has died in child-birth or of the man who has been slain by a wild beast, are often regarded as specially malignant and dangerous.

Mr. Fryer mentions how, in his district, the spirit of a man slain by a tiger was propitiated for ten or twelve days after his death. The chief aim of the propitiatory rites seems to have been to bring the spirit away from the tiger to its old home. A thread was tied to a beam, and a copper ring was attached to it by twisting a thread round it without a knot. Below was placed a pot full of water. Songs were sung, and watch was kept by day and by night, until the ring at last fell into the water, thereby announcing that the spirit had escaped from his captor, and had returned to his family.

CHAPTER XIV

A FEW WORDS ON MISSION WORK IN GONDWANA

WE have endeavoured to give some kind of picture of Gondwana in the more primitive days of its old Gond rulers. We have seen it in its unhappiness and unrest, and under the uncertain and oft-times rapacious grasp of Maratha rule. We see it to-day enjoying peace and increasing prosperity, under the mild and just rule of Great Britain. If we have dwelt a little on the work of some of our leading administrators who have helped to bring in this new and better order of things, it is but natural that we should make some reference to those high-souled men and women, who have striven to establish Christ's Kingdom in these regions.

The missionary problems in the Central Provinces are in some respects unlike those which obtain in most other parts of India. The Mohammedan population is, with the exception of Berar, neither large nor influential, the large Hindu population is in many parts still largely illiterate, and we have well over two million aboriginal Gonds, not to speak of other tribes of aborigines, Kols, Kurkus, and Merias.

One or two of the missionary bodies at work in Gondwana have been working for more than two

ALL SAINTS' CATHEDRAL, NAGPUR

generations, others have only recently entered this part of the mission field.

Of those who have been at work in the southern part of Gondwana from the days when Bhonslas reigned in Nagpur, the United Free Church of Scotland clearly takes the most prominent place. Ever since the days when Stephen Hislop, that many-sided missionary, laboured indefatigably in this part of India, the United Free Church of Scotland has sent out a succession of able men and devoted women to carry on the work so well started by its pioneer missionaries. No one who lives in Nagpur can fail to observe the important place which this mission fills in the life of the large native city and the surrounding country. Year after year, for more than a generation past, its University College, appropriately named after Hislop, its most distinguished missionary, has been sending out numbers of highly-educated Indian youths, to fill various offices in our public life. Nor has any medical mission in all India done more valuable work than the medical branch of this mission, with its excellent women's hospital and its admirable staff of lady doctors and nurses.

Nor can anyone who lives in Nagpur be blind to the great devotion of the large body of Roman Catholic priests and sisters, who are working under their own Bishop, many of them connected with the mission of St. Francis de Sales.

And if Scotland and France have sent many devoted sons and daughters to missionary work in Gondwana, many a small mission station dotted about in the beautiful Satpura country speaks no less eloquently of the devotion of the Scandinavian Church of Sweden.

Nor, too, does Europe alone share all the burden of missionary enterprise in this part of India, for to-day with their headquarters at Jubbulpore, both the American Methodist Episcopal Church and the American Baptist Society are throwing out branches of their work, with characteristic energy, all over this large area.

While it is obviously impossible in the limits of one short chapter to enter fully even into the work of those missions with which the writer is personally connected, there are some facts connected with our Church Missionary Society's work amongst the Gonds, which seem to me to fit in admirably with the general purpose of our story, and to throw interesting light on some aspects of missionary effort.

Few, however doubtful or unsympathetic as to missionary work amongst the highly educated Hindus or Mohammedans, will ever raise any opposition to the Church's endeavour to evangelise the devil-worshipping aborigines. The late Sir Charles Elliott, when Lieutenant-Governor of Bengal, speaking of missionary work in India, dwelt especially on the importance of work amongst the aborigines, and added that there was no sphere in which the great truths of Christianity, more especially the Fatherhood of God, seemed to find a more congenial soil than amongst those spiritually degraded devil-worshippers. I can myself recall a conversation I had years ago with a Mohammedan gentleman of Delhi; and how, after describing our missionary labours amongst the aborigines of Chhota Nagpur, he stated how willingly he would assist in a work of teaching them about the true God!

Curiously enough the first Christian mission to the Gonds was started, and largely supported, by one who, in after years, became a distinguished Indian administrator, and who finished his career as Lieutenant-Governor of the Punjab.

In the year 1831 Mr. Donald McLeod was appointed to the Department for the suppression of Thuggee under the superintendence of Colonel W. Sleeman, and was stationed at Saugor. Shortly afterwards he was transferred to Seoni as Deputy Commissioner, where he remained for several years. During this time he formed the deepest affection for this beautiful Satpura district and for the simple-minded Gonds. So strongly did this fancy grow, that at one time he even wished to spend the remainder of his career among the Gonds, and declined several better appointments in other parts of the country. He writes from Seoni in the following strain—

"I look upon my lot as fixed in this country, a land of wondrous interest, albeit at present in the darkness of night."

A few years later, in 1840, Mr. McLeod was appointed to Jubbulpore as Deputy Commissioner. It was then that he carried out his long-conceived plan of commencing a Christian mission among the Gonds. "He had long felt," so his biographer tells us, "that the simple habits of this primitive race afforded an admirable field for Christian effort, and he had for some time past endeavoured to enlist the sympathy and co-operation of Christian people at Calcutta and elsewhere, in his cherished project. He had written a long and interesting article on this subject in the *Calcutta Christian Observer*, in which he endeavoured to show that the best plan was to start an agricultural mission settlement amongst them."

As no English Missionary Society was willing to take up this idea, he acted upon it himself, and applied to Pastor Gossner, of Berlin, who sent out to him a little band of German artisans and husbandmen (a carpenter, a schoolmaster, and an apothecary were amongst the number) to work among the Gonds. They were placed under the superintendence of the Rev. Alois Loesch, a Lutheran Minister, who had previously worked in South India.

The missionary band arrived at Jubbulpore in 1841, and shortly afterwards proceeded to the Satpura Highlands, making their central station at the village of Karanjia, in the Mandla district, about fourteen miles from the source of the Nerbudda at Amarkantak. There they lived in a simple fashion, building their bungalow with their own hands.

Shortly after their arrival at Karanjia, Mr. McLeod was able to pay them a visit. He was delighted at what appeared to be the happy commencement of favourable mission work amongst the Gonds.

We have a few interesting lines from the pen of the leader of this missionary enterprise, the Rev. A. Loesch, which were written at this period—

"Karanjia is one of the finest places I have seen in India. It is sixteen miles to the west of Amarkantak, and situated on the road to that place; it is often visited by hosts of fakirs and ghosains,[1] who extort the last coin from the poor ignorant Gonds, whom we shall no longer suffer to be maltreated by that idle and wicked set of people. The climate is almost European, the soil very fertile and the water delicious."

The first few months had passed, and the sky seemed unclouded, when there fell on this small missionary band a calamity as sudden as it was terrible. Early in the rains an epidemic of cholera swept over this neighbourhood, and within a few weeks four of the mission band were dead, and a fifth lay between life and death. The doctor was unfortunately the first to die, and this fact may have been partly responsible for the

[1] Religious mendicants.

death of the others. One of the survivors lost his reason, and died not long afterwards, the other joined Stephen Hislop in Nagpur and died three years later. Within a few months of its starting, the mission had ceased to exist.

In the winter of 1903, I paid my first visit to the Mandla district, to visit our Church Missionary Society's mission stations. On my way to Amarkantak I determined to visit Karanjia, the scene of this tragedy. On arriving at the village my companions and I found the grave of these four German missionaries in a deplorable state. The stone cross which had stood at the head had been maliciously broken by a Mohammedan fanatic. This mutilated grave alone remained to mark where these good men had lived and died.

At my suggestion my companion, the Rev. H. Molony, now Bishop of Chehkiang in China, wrote a short pamphlet called *A Forgotten Tragedy*, describing the death of these devoted men. Later on we took steps to have the grave repaired, when we placed a solid iron Maltese cross horizontally on the slab which covers the grave. On each arm of the cross is inscribed the name of one of the four departed missionaries—the Rev. Alois Loesch, Julius Schleisner, Karl Gatzky, and Heinrich Gossner. Underneath are written in the Hindi language the beautiful words, "Blessed are the dead which die in the Lord."

Such was the hard fate which befell Mr. McLeod's endeavours to establish a mission amongst the

THE LONELY GRAVE AT KARANJIA

Gonds. That it should have ended with such tragic suddenness is all the more mysterious when one reflects on the remarkable results achieved by Pastor Gossner's mission in Chhota Nagpur, a mission which was established a few years later.

Within a year or two of this tragedy, Mr. McLeod was transferred to Benares, and later on to the Punjab, where in due course he became Lieutenant-Governor of the Punjab. How highly the Sikhs of the Punjab esteemed his noble and devout character may be seen in our illustration, which represents him, at a later stage of his career, being worshipped by an adoring body of Sikhs.

After Mr. McLeod's departure nothing was done to evangelise the Gonds for some years. Ten years later, another civilian, Mr. Mosley Smith, then Sessions Judge of Jubbulpore, in consultation with Mr. Dawson, the Chaplain of Jubbulpore, obtained from the Church Missionary Society the funds necessary to support a missionary sent out by Pastor Gossner. The name of this missionary was the Rev. J. W. Rebsch. Later on the Rev. E. C. Stuart (afterwards the Bishop of Waiapu in New Zealand) was for a time stationed by the Church Missionary Society in Jubbulpore, and did some work amongst the Gonds.

Not, however, until the arrival of the Rev. E. Champion, in 1860, was work pressed on with full vigour. During the twenty-one years of Mr. Champion's labours in this part of India he accomplished a great deal. Of the many boys trained in an orphanage which he started at Chiriadongree, near Mandla, one, the Rev. Failbus, was destined to be the first Indian clergyman in the Gond mission.

Towards the end of Mr. Champion's period the Rev. H. D. Williamson joined the mission, and laid the main foundations of the existing work amongst the Gonds of the Mandla district. The Gondi language was, under his guidance, reduced to writing, and a Hindi grammar and vocabulary were prepared by him. Portions of the New Testament and numerous Bible stories were translated into Gondi. A valuable hymn book was also translated by him into Hindi, a language understood by most of the Gonds in the Satpuras.

The story of Mr. Williamson's first Gond convert is so typical of the earliest stage in conversion amongst some of the most spiritual of our aboriginal Christians, that I venture to tell it, very much as it is told in Mr. Fryer's little book, *The Story of the Gond Mission*

Bhoi Baba was the head-man of a village, and "a devotee." His reputation for religious devotion was widespread. He had learnt to read, and was in the habit of spending long periods in meditation. On one occasion he spent weeks meditating on a huge rock in the middle of a river, and on another spent a similar period under a large pipal tree in his own village.

Hearing of his devotion, Mr. Williamson

REVERENCE OF A SECT OF SIKHS FOR SIR D. McLEOD

determined to visit him in his village. On the day of his arrival, however, at the Bhoi's village, he heard with deep regret that the Bhoi was absent, and would not be back for days. Much to his surprise and delight, however, shortly before night fell, the Bhoi walked into his village. Nor was Mr. Williamson's delight lessened when the Bhoi told him "that when he had travelled about ten miles from his village, something had said to him, "Go back to your village at once."

Then began a course of instruction which led to his conversion and baptism a few months later.

Since Mr. Williamson's departure from the mission several missionaries of our Church have worked in this district for longer or shorter periods. It is interesting to note that two of their number, the Rev. H. P. Parker and the Rev. H. Molony, were taken from this jungle mission to fill important missionary bishoprics in other parts of the world.

The Rev. H. P. Parker, after a short period of service in the Mandla district, was appointed as successor to Bishop Hannington, the Martyr Bishop of Uganda. Unfortunately on his way from the coast to his diocese, in the heart of Africa, he contracted fever and died before reaching Uganda. The other missionary to the Gonds similarly honoured was the Rev. Herbert Molony, now Bishop of Chehkiang in China. With deep devotion he laboured for many years amongst the Gonds. During his period stations were opened at Marpha in the heart of the district, and at Sukulpura, on the banks of the Nerbudda, at the edge of the Rewah State.

This mission is, indeed, full of promise, if only more workers of the right kind can be found for it. One of its greatest needs is a medical missionary, and another is a missionary with a practical knowledge of farming. Whether one sees it at Patpara, with its schools, orphanage, and leper settlement, at present under the management of the Rev. J. Wakeling; or at its little agricultural settlement at Deori, where Mr. and Mrs. Charles are working; or away in the heart of the jungle at Marpha, where for years past the Rev. E. D. Price (beloved of the Gonds) has been living, one can easily understand the feelings which Sir Donald McLeod felt in days gone by for these people, and their beautiful jungle country.

It would be an easy and a pleasant task to tell something of the excellent missionary work which is being carried on by our Church in Jubbulpore and Katni, under the guidance of the Rev. Canon E. A. Hensley, Secretary of the Church Missionary Society. In such a description, were I to attempt it, some mention would have to be made of the fine Church Missionary Society High School in Jubbulpore for boys, and the excellent Church of England Zenana Missionary Society High School for girls in Katni, started a few years ago by Miss J. Bardsley. But as I have felt it wiser to limit myself almost exclusively to work

MARPHA MISSIONARY SETTLEMENT

amongst the Gonds, I will, before concluding, turn my readers' attention, for a moment or two, to our work amongst the Gonds in the Chanda district.

It is interesting to note that the mission at Chanda, like more than one mission of our Church in India, owes its commencement to an Indian chaplain. In the year 1870, when Chaplain of Nagpur, the Rev. G. T. Carruthers first urged the claims of India on the Episcopal Church of Scotland. Hitherto that Church had directed its foreign missionary efforts almost exclusively to work in South Africa.

The earlier efforts of the Chanda mission were carried on largely by Indian workers. For a time the saintly Father Nehemiah Goreh, commonly called "Nilkant Shastri," a converted Maratha Brahmin, worked in Chanda. As one who can recall his unique personality, I appreciate deeply Canon Wood's description of Nehemiah Goreh's work and influence in Chanda. Of him he writes—

"His memory is still green. I have heard from many lips the tale of his argument with Pilba, the Guru of the Kabir Panthis, of his casting down of the god of the Mahars, that stood on the wall by the Pathanpura gate, and thereby converting one family, and frightening another family, so that they fled to the Nizam's dominion to escape the wrath of that god, and have not returned to this place. . . But the story that I like best of all is how he used to preach in the bazaar. They tell of him as a slim figure dressed in a white cassock. Round his neck was a rosary of wooden beads, and attached to it a wooden cross. In his hand he held a heavy wooden cross, that stood higher than his head, and on this he leaned. People passed and re-passed going about their business, but he stood still, taking no notice of them whatever. But as he stood silent there, for an hour, perhaps, or more, the people noted, watched, stood around at a distance, waiting shyly, for whether he were a Christian or not, at least he was a Brahmin. Then, at last, when a circle had gathered round him in the cool of the evening, he preached to them of Christ."

Under his saintly influence the mission grew, and when he left Chanda in 1874 he had already gathered out from heathenism a small body of Christians. Then for twenty years the mission was entrusted to the care of the Rev. Israel Jacob, until the arrival of the Rev. A. Wood in December, 1898. From that time forward the work of the mission has gone on steadily and strongly, until it has gained a real place in the life and affection of the people of the old Gond capital and its surrounding country. Assisted by his colleagues, the Rev. G. D. Philip, the Rev. J. R. McKenzie, and by some devoted lady workers, schools and orphanages have been started, a mission church built and consecrated, fresh stations created, and an important branch of work opened in Nagpur itself.

In a charming little book, called *In and Out of*

PATPARA LEPER SETTLEMENT

Chanda, we have a most interesting account of this mission, mainly from the writings of Canon Wood.

Looking back over the years which have passed since my Consecration in 1903, I recall no happier days than those I have spent during my visits to our missions amongst the Gonds in the Mandla district and in Chanda.

My task is now completed, but, ere I bring my story of Gondwana to a conclusion, I would say one or two words on behalf of the aim of all true missionary enterprise in India.

It is little more than fifty years since the great John Lawrence, when speaking of mission work, told the people of England that "Christian truths taught in a Christian way will never offend the people of India."

There is a hard and unsympathetic way of approaching those from whom we differ, which is certain to stir up bitterness and angry feeling; but the simple presentation of the Life and Teaching of Christ by men and women who are endeavouring to imitate His supreme example, in lives of lowly service, kindliness, and self-sacrifice, can never produce anything save feelings of respect and admiration amongst the masses of India, who are essentially religious.

But there is one aspect of the missionary message which may well be considered by a people like the English, on whom imperial and wide-world responsibilities are laid. Never was the teaching of Christ about the brotherhood of man more needed than it is to-day. We have seen what terrible evils an exaggerated patriotism may bring on the world. What the world most needs to-day is the Divine Spirit of love and brotherhood, which can draw the various races of mankind together, and can make them realise that not in envy and hatred, and not in an endeavour to destroy one another, but in mutual co-operation and goodwill lie the highest and deepest interests, as well as the truest and noblest life for all mankind.

CHAPTER XV

THE STORY OF LINGO

Ye who love a Nation's legends,
Love the ballads of a people,
That like voices from afar off
Call to us to pause and listen,
Speak in tones so plain and childlike,
Scarcely can the ear distinguish
Whether they are sung or spoken:—
Listen to this Indian legend.

—LONGFELLOW.

No account of the Gonds would be complete without some reference to the quaint songs which link themselves with the name of Lingo, the Gond prophet, and which form a sort of Epic once recited by Gond Pardhans, or Bards. This Epic for so we may style it, was first brought to light half a century ago, by the Rev. S. Hislop, one of the pioneer missionaries of the last century. Hislop in his wanderings amongst the Gonds, and in his researches into things Gondian, first heard of it from one of their Pardhans, or Bards. He reduced it to writing in the Gondi language with his own hand shortly before his too early and tragic death; and the task of having it translated, first into Hindi, and afterwards into English, was carried out under the direction of his friend, Sir R. Temple, the Chief Commissioner of the

Central Provinces. The English translation as it is found in these pages is that of Sir R. Temple himself, which is in every way to be preferred to a paraphrase cast in the metre of Longfellow's "Hiawatha," by Captain Forsyth in *The Highlands of Central India.* Reading it for the first time in Forsyth's paraphrase and with his not very sympathetic comments fresh in my mind, I was certainly not prepared for the quaint humour and real charm revealed in Sir R. Temple's translation.

This Epic, as Sir R. Temple truly says, is "a compendium of Gond thoughts and notions." Though abounding in things borrowed from the Hindus, it is possessed of real originality, and in many passages steeped with Gond ideas. It was customary for Gond Pardhans to recite it to circles of listening Gonds at marriages, and on other festive occasions. Now that under changed conditions of Gond life it is seldom if ever heard (it is, I am told, quite unknown in most parts of modern Gondwana), it is well that Hislop's interesting discovery should be rescued from the oblivion into which it has undoubtedly fallen.

As to how old this story of Lingo really is, no one can say. One or two scholars with higher critical tendencies have suggested that it is possibly of Brahmanic origin, and that it may have been foisted on the Gonds for the purpose of popularising amongst them the worship of Shiva. Sir R. Temple in his editorial notes expresses the view that though the original form must be quite ancient, yet the framework of the story, as it now exists, was clearly composed after the arrival of the Aryans amongst the aborigines in Central India. The Epic was never written, and the modern Gond Pardhans, being unlettered men, do not attempt to explain its history.

Sir R. Temple divides it into five parts. Such a division is a good way of reminding the modern reader that it was probably sung or recited in parts. It is also a convenient way of separating the various subjects treated in the Epic.

Part I —deals with the creation of the Gond people and their subsequent bondage.

Part II —tells of the birth, life and death of the mythical hero, the Prophet Lingo.

Part III —deals with the revival of Lingo and his delivery of the Gonds from bondage.

Part IV —deals with the sub-division of the Gonds into tribes and the institution of the worship of the Gonds.

Part V —deals with the institution of the rites of marriage amongst the Gonds by Lingo.

As Sir R. Temple's translation fills many pages, it is necessary for us to omit considerable portions of it, and to confine ourselves to its more interesting parts, especially those which throw light on Gond customs.

PART I

THE CREATION OF THE GOND PEOPLE AND THEIR SUBSEQUENT BONDAGE

THE history opens in the silence and solitude of the glens of the seven hills, which are clearly the Satpura Mountains of the Central Provinces.

In the midst of twelve hills, in the glens of seven hills, is Lingan, or Mount Lingana.

In the Mount is a flower tree named Dăti. Thence for twelve leagues (kôss) there are no dwellers.

Caw says there is no crow, chirp says there is no bird, roar says there is no tiger.

Then follows a weird passage (in which Hindu ideas are clearly predominant), which describes the process by which the Gond people were created.

The god Mahadeva performs an act of penance (tăp) which lasts for twelve months. At the end of the period, one, Kalia Adao, the Divine Ancestor of the Gonds, is born " from a boil in Mahadeva's hand." Kalia Adao in his turn performs an act of penance (tăp), and from a boil in his own hand sixteen daughters are born. He is bitterly disappointed. Daughters are regarded by him, as by so many Indians, as by no means a blessing.

"What! Why are these daughters born? I shall have cause to cast my head down. When shall I bring husbands for them?"

He took hold of them, and threw them in the water. After throwing them into it the water dried up, and sixteen sorts of earth were produced.

After this rather drastic way of disposing of his sixteen daughters who, the Pardhan explained to Hislop, were goddesses from whose remains the several soils known to Gonds were made (black cotton, reddish earth, sandy ground, murrum, gravel, etc.), Kalia Adao began a second penance (tăp). On this occasion he was more successful. From it "twelve threshing-floors of Gondi gods were born." These are the ancestors of the Gond race.

Then follows an amusing description of the wild Gonds in their primitive state. Ignorant, dirty, madly fond of sport, they incur the displeasure of the great god Mahadeva, who, by an ingenious and most ungod-like trick, lures them, like the Pied Piper of Hamlin, into a vast cave, where they are incarcerated. A giant Bhasmasur stands guard over it. Four Gonds, however, more slow of foot than their brethren, remain outside. Parvati, the wife of Mahadeva and a lover of the Gonds, is in deep distress at their disappearance. She commences an act of devotion (tăp) and at the end of it the high god, Bhagawan, says that he will again make her Gonds visible.

Twelve threshing-floors[1] of Gondi gods[2] were born.

Hither and thither all the Gonds were scattered in the jungle.

Places, hills, and valleys, were filled with these Gonds.

Even trees had their Gonds. How did the Gonds conduct themselves ?

Whatever came across them they must needs kill and eat it.

They made no distinction. If they saw a jackal they killed and ate it.

No distinction was observed; they respected not antelope, sambhar, and the like.

They made no distinction in eating a sow, a quail, a pigeon, a crow, a kite, an adjutant, a vulture:

A lizard, a frog, a beetle, a cow, a calf, a he- and she-buffalo:

Rats, bandicoots, squirrels—all these they killed and ate.

So began the Gonds to do. They devoured raw and ripe things.

They did not bathe for six months together.

They did not wash their faces properly, even on dung-hills they would fall down and remain.

Such were the Gonds born in the beginning. A smell was spread over the jungle.

When the Gonds were thus disorderly behaved: they became disagreeable to Mahadeva.

[1] The threshing-floor is one of the most important places in Indian village life.

[2] The original Gonds are spoken of as "gods."

EPIC OF LINGO—"THE SQUIRREL RAN AND THEY PURSUED IT"

Who said, "The caste of the Gonds is very bad.

"I will not preserve them; they will ruin my hill Dhawalagiri.

"I perceive here and there smells." So said Mahadeva. "Call the Gonds."

So said he to Narayan. He went, and called them.

And brought them into the presence of Mahadeva.

When they were standing Mahadeva arose and looked and saw all the Gonds come.

He spoke within himself, and took them away into his valley.

He made them to sit in a line, and he sat at the head of them.

He took substance from his own body, and made it into a squirrel.

Thus he made a squirrel while bathing, and gave it life.

When he made it alive, he caused it to run away.

With its upright tail the squirrel ran from the midst of them.

The Gonds saw it running, and they pursued it.

As the Gonds were pursuing it, some said, "Kill it, kill it!"

Another said, "Catch it; it will serve as a nice roast."

So saying some seized a stick, some a stone.

Some seized a clod; their waist-cloths were shaking; their hair began to fly about.

The squirrel entered a hole, which was the god's prison on earth.

The Gonds also followed it up to the hole.

All the threshing-floor[1] Gonds ran into the cave.

Thus all the Gonds ran; the rest, four[2] in number, remained behind.

They came to Parvati; she was sleeping. In the meantime she awoke. She cared for the Gonds. She said, "For many days I have not seen my Gonds.

"There used to be noise in mount Dhawalagiri.

"But to-day there is silence. For many days there has been a smell (of Gonds).

"But to-day I perceive no smell.

"They must have gone somewhere.

"Mahadeva is not to be seen, where did he lead them?" Thus said Parvati.

She ascended Dhawalagiri, and saw no Gonds. Then she said to Mahadeva, "My Gonds do not appear, where have they gone?"

Mahadeva arose and placed a stone sixteen cubits long at the entrance of the cave, and thus shut in the Gonds.

He stationed Bhasmasur,[3] a giant, to guard it. Still Parvati remained asking after them.

Then said Mahadeva, "Dhawalagiri began to be odorous, and I fell into a rage thereat.

[1] See note on line 11. The term "threshing-floor Gonds" means the regular Gonds created by Mahadeva.

[2] The number of four persons, which appears in subsequent parts of the story, might be thought to have some significance, but none is ascertainable.

[3] This Bhasmasur was one of the giants of Hindu mythology, who got from Shiva power to reduce to ashes all whom he touched. He became so troublesome that Shiva, in self-defence, had to kill him.

"But four Gonds have survived, and they are fled." So said he.

Then Parvati thought in her mind, "My Gonds are lost."

. . . . . .

The four Gonds who fled travelled onward over hills.

Thence they went and saw a tree rising upright, as Date tree.

Which they climbed, and looked about them.

They said, "There is no hiding place visible for us."

But one of them looked and saw a place named Kachikopa[1] Lahugad.

They went by the jungle road and reached that place.

There the four brothers remained.

When the Gonds were not to be found, Parvati began to feel regret for them.

She then commenced a devotion (tăp).

Six months passed.

Parvati ended her tăp. Bhagawan[2] (god) meanwhile was swinging in a swing.

[1] The name Kachikopa Lahugad appears frequently in the story, but there is no known place particularly of that name. The meaning in Gondi is the " Iron Valley—the Red Hills," a nomenclature very applicable to the mineral products and external aspect of many hills in the Gonds' country.

[2] The name god Bhagawan occurs frequently in all the Parts. It is borrowed, of course, from Hinduism. It is remarkable that this name should be used, as the Gonds give the name of Bara Deo to the one great God, supreme over all the gods. The name Bara Deo is found nowhere in these songs.

He said, "What devotee at my resting time has begun a devotion?

"Narayan, go and see to it."

Narayan went to see; ascending a hill, he came to Parvati. And stood while Parvati was performing her tăp, and saying, "My threshing-floor Gonds do not appear.

"Therefore I commenced my devotion." When Narayan heard this he ran; resting and running, he came to Bhagawan and said, "Parvati is performing a devotion, and says my threshing-floor Gonds do not appear; where have they gone?"

Bhagawan said, "Go and tell her, I will make her Gonds visible."

Part II

THE BIRTH, LIFE AND DEATH OF LINGO

> There he sang of Hiawatha,
> Sang his wondrous birth and being,
> How he lived, and toiled and suffered,
> That he might advance his people.
>
> —Longfellow.

The Gond race is embowelled in the earth. Only four Gonds remain outside. Bhagawan, the high god, had promised the goddess Parvati, Mahadeva's wife, to rescue them from their incarceration. This is the state of things when the second part of the poem begins. Amid the same scenes of silence and solitude, described for us in the opening lines of the Epic, there stood a flower tree called Dăti. By the decree of Bhagawan from one of the flowers of this tree was to spring one "without father or mother" who was to be the teacher and civiliser of the Gonds, and eventually their deliverer from Mahadeo's cruel incarceration. His name is Lingo. Though he appears throughout the poem in the character of a Hindu saint, the name is said to be of Gond origin. Sometimes he is called Bhan (Gondi for devotee) and sometimes Pariur (Gondi for saint).

In one passage Lingo is spoken of as a pure and sinless being. "Lingo was a perfect man ; water may be stained, but he had no stain whatever."

Then care fell to Bhagawan (god), There was a tree.

It was blossoming. Then, said he, "One of its flowers shall conceive."

By God's doing, clouds and winds were loosed. A cloud

Like a fan arose; thunder roared, and lightning flashed.

The flower burst, clouds opened, and darkness fell; the day was hid.

A heap of turmeric fell at the fourth watch of the night.

In the morning, when clouds resounded with thunder, the flower opened

And burst, and Lingo was born, and he sprang, and fell into the heap of turmeric.

Then the clouds cleared, and at the dawn Lingo began to cry.

Thereat, care fell upon God; the (face of Lingo) began to dry amidst the powder.

But by God's doing, there was a fig tree, on which was honey.

The honey burst, and a small drop fell into his mouth.

Thus the juice continued to fall, and his mouth began to suck.

It was noon, and wind blew, when Lingo began to grow.

He leapt into a swing, and began to swing, when day was set

Lingo arose with haste, and sat in a cradle swinging.

BIRTH OF LINGO—"THE FLOWER OPENED"

THE STORY OF LINGO

Lingo was a perfect man; water may be stained but he had no stain whatever.

There was a diamond on his navel, and sandal wood mark on his forehead. He was a divine saint. He became two years old.

He played in turmeric, and slept in a swing. Thus days rolled away.

He became nine years old; he was ordered not to eat anything from off the jungle trees, or thickets.

Lingo's childhood and youth were spent Pan-like in absolute solitude. He craved for the society of other men like himself. Filled with this desire he set out on a journey which led him to Kachikopa Lahugad—"The Iron Valley—the Red Hills," an admirable description of many of the hills of the Satpuras—with their red rocks abounding in manganese ore. Here he sees for the first time his fellow-men, who turn out to be the four surviving Gonds.

Lingo, in his mind, said, "Here is no person to be seen; man does not appear, neither are there any animals.

"There appears none like me; I will go where I can see someone like myself."

Having said so, one day he arose and went on straight.

He ascended a needle-like hill; there he saw a Mundita tree;

Below was a tree named Kidsadita; it blossomed.

He went thither, and having seen flowers, he smelled them.

He went a little beyond, upon a precipitous hill, and climbed a tree.

Then he looked around and saw smoke arising from Kachikopa Lahugad.

"What is this ?" said he ; "I must go and see it."

He ascended, and saw the smoke. The four brothers quickly brought their game, and began to roast it ; they began to eat it raw or cooked.

In the meantime Lingo went there. They saw him and stood up ; he stood also ;

Neither spoke to the other. The four then began to say within themselves,

"We are four brothers, and he will be the fifth brother. Let us call him.

"We will go and bring him." Then they went.

They came to the place where he was. "Who art thou ?" asked they of Lingo.

Lingo said, "I am Saint Lingo ; I have a knot of hair on my head."

The four brothers said, "Come to our house."

They took him home. Some game was lying there.

Then follows an amusing description of Lingo joining these four Gonds in their favourite pastime of hunting. The hunt is for an animal "without a liver," which, needless to say, was never found.

Lingo said, "What is this ?" They said, "It is game that we have brought."

"What kind of game is this?" Lingo asked. They said, "It is a pig."

He said, "Give me its liver." There was no liver there. Then they said,

"Hear, O brother, we have killed an animal without liver!"

Then Lingo said, "Let me see an animal without liver."

Then care fell upon them. "Where shall we show him an animal without a liver?" said they.

One said, "Hear my word! He is a little fellow, we are big men; we will take him to the jungle among large stones.

"Among thorns in thickets and caves we will roam; he will get tired, and will sit down;

"He will be thirsty and hungry, then he will propose to return."

With Lingo they, with bow and arrow in their hands, went by the jungle road.

Onward they went, and saw an antelope. Lingo said, "Kill it!"

It had a liver. Then came a sambhar, "Kill ye it!"

It had a liver. A hare came, and he said, "Kill ye it!"

It had a liver.

Thus the devout Lingo did not tire. These four brothers were tired.

For water they thirsted. On a steep they ascended to look for water;

But no water appeared, so they descended from the hill.

Thus they came to a thick jungle of Anjun trees where thorny plants blocked the road.

They came and stood. A little water appeared. They plucked Palas (Butia) leaves, and made them into a trough;

They drank water with it, and were much refreshed.

Lingo said, "What are you doing sitting there?"

They said, "We cannot find an animal without a liver."

Then follows a description of a very ancient and primitive method of cultivation, which is still practised by Gonds, and other aborigines, in the hilly and forest parts of India. A piece of forest land on a hill-side is selected. The trees at the edge of the forest are cut down, and set fire to. When the monsoon-rains come, the ashes of these trees are washed over the soil near this forest, and on this land manured with nothing save these ashes, and over which no plough has passed, the seed is sown. An abundant crop is the result. This land is sown again the next year, but with diminishing result. It is then abandoned for twelve years, during which period the Gonds think it will have recovered its strength, and again be able to yield crops. Such a method of cultivation, called "Dhaya," is obviously most destructive to forests; and as the ashes of the teak tree are especially fertilising, it is certain that many a tract of country in the Central Provinces has been deprived of its noble teak forests by the Gonds, in their laziness and ignorance. The verses below describe the cutting down of the forest trees preparatory to burning them.

They went aside and sat down. Then arose Lingo and held a hatchet in his hand;

And went on cutting trees; the trees fell, their roots were dug up.

Thus he began to cut down jungles. In an hour he made a good field.

They said, "Our hands are blistered, and not one tree have we cut down.

"But Lingo in one hour has cut down several trees;

"He has made the black soil appear, and has sown rice and hedged it round;

"He has made a door to it, and has made a shutter for the door."

Then they arose and took their homeward road, and came to their own houses.

On the first day of the rainy season a little black cloud appeared.

Wind blew violently; it was cloudy all day; rain began to fall.

Rills in the open places were filled knee-deep; all the holes were filled with water.

When the rain had poured for three days, the weather became fair; rice began to spring;

All the fields appeared green. In one day the rice grew a finger's breadth high;

In a month it rose up to a man's knee.

Then follows a charming passage describing how a herd of deer or nilgai (blue bull) visit the crops so recently sown by Lingo, and eat the young rice. The Gonds, on returning to their fields, find their crops eaten, and filled with anger, pursue the deer under the guidance of Lingo. Two only of the herd escape.

There were sixteen scores of nilgais or deer, among whom two bucks, uncle and nephew, were chiefs.

When the scent of rice spread around, they came to know it; thither they went to graze.

At the head of the herd was the uncle, and the nephew was at the rear.

With cracking joints the nephew arose; he leaped upwards.

With two ears upright, and with cheerful heart, he bounded towards his uncle.

And said, "Someone has a beautiful field of rice: it must be green tender fodder.

"To us little ones give that field, the sixteen scores of deer will go there;

"After eating rice we will come back." The uncle said, "O nephew, hear my words! Take

"The name of the field, but not that of Lingo's field,

"Otherwise he will not preserve even one of the sixteen scores of deer for seed to carry on the race."

The nephew said, "You are old, but we are young; we will go.

"Arriving there we will eat. If any one sees us we will bound away;

"We will make a jump of five cubits, and thus escape; but you, being an old one, will be caught.

"Therefore you are afraid to go, I will not hear your word; don't come with us."

So said the nephew. With straight tails and erect ears they turned back.

The uncle was grieved. Then he arose and went after them;

They left him far behind. The herd came near the fields;

But the nephew and the deer began to look for a way to enter it, but could not find one.

The deer said, "Your uncle was the wise one amongst us, of whom shall we now ask advice?

"We have left him behind; instead of him, you are our chief."

The nephew said, "Do as you see me doing before you."

He put himself in front, when one of the deer said

At first, "Your uncle told you that this is Lingo's field, but you did not hear;

"Look behind and before you; be prudent." So said the deer.

But the nephew said, "We will not keep an old one's company."

So he, being in front, gave a bound, and was in the midst of the rice,

And stood; then all the deer came after him leaping.

After him came the uncle to the hedge and stood.

All the deer were eating rice. But the uncle could not find his way.

Being old, he was unable to leap the door of the field of rice.

They went from thence and leaped back over the hedge, when the uncle said to them—

"Hear, O sixteen scores of deer, you have eaten this field!

"Father Lingo, when he comes to it,

"What measures will he adopt?" Then the nephew, who was behind, came in front,

And said, "Hear, O friends and brethren! flee from this place but hear my word.

"As you flee, keep your feet on leaves, and stones, and boughs, and grass, but don't put your feet on the soil."

So said the nephew.

As he told them so they did—all the sixteen scores of deer began to run,

And left no mark nor traces.

Then they stopped: some remained standing, some slept.

In the midst of the flower fragrance was Lingo sleeping, while half of the night was passed.

In his dream he saw a field eaten by deer, and all the rice becoming spoilt.

Then Lingo departed, and took his road to Kachikopa Lahugad.

Hence he departed, and went to the brothers and said, "O brothers! out of your house come ye;

"Hear one word: the deer have eaten our field of rice."

The four brothers said, "We need rice to offer our first-fruits to the gods."

Then Lingo said, "Hear, O brethren! our rice has been eaten up;

"It has spoilt; we have no first-fruits." Lingo said, "We will offer the liver of these deer as first-fruits;

"Then I will remain as a devotee, otherwise my power will vanish.

"I will fill my stomach by the smelling of flowers;

"But how will the Gonds fill their bellies, there is nothing for their eating—

"The rice has been spoilt by the deer." So said Lingo.

The four brothers said, "We will take in our arms bow and arrow."

With anger against the deer they came to the field, and entered in the midst of it.

When they came in the centre they saw only black soil.

Only rice stubble appeared, and Lingo saw nothing.

Then his anger arose from the heel to the head, and he bit his finger on the spot;

His eyes became red. "Where are the deer?" said he, "look for them."

They looked, but did not see anywhere the footprints of deer.

Near a tree they beheld some foot-marks: they looked at it.

As they went they beheld a jungle trodden down; then some traces appeared.

Onward they went, but did not see the deer, they beheld a Peepul tree.

Lingo said, "I will climb the tree, you stand below."

From the top he looked, and the deer were visible. He said,

"The deer are in sight, some are seated, some are sleeping, some are leaping about.

"You four brothers separate yourselves on four sides with your arrows,

"And allow not one of the deer to escape.

"I will shoot them from the tree, and you shoot from below."

Having heard this, the four brothers went and ambuscaded on four sides.

They shot their arrows from four corners, while Lingo shot from the tree.

The uncle, the buck, and one deer alone survived; they had aimed at them also, but the arrow fell from Lingo's hand.

He said to himself, "When the arrow fell out of my hand, that must have been a good omen,

"That uncle is a devout follower of the servant of god, he has not eaten anything."

But the two survivors began to run; then these four brothers went after them in pursuit, saying, "We will catch them here or there."

But the two could not be found; then the brothers turned and looked around.
The eldest brother said, "Hear, O brethren! These two have escaped, and Lingo
"Has remained behind at a distance from us. Let us return," said the eldest brother.
When they returned, Lingo asked them, "Where have you been?"
They said, "The two survivors have fled and cannot be found, so we have returned to you."

Then Lingo tried to teach the primitive Gonds how to obtain fire by means of flint. His lesson was not very successful, and as his four disciples had never seen fire, he told them that living just three kōss (six miles) is a giant named Rikad Gawadi, in whose field they will see fire, that great gift of the gods to man.

It has been suggested by Sir R. Temple in his editorial notes that the name Gawadi may be a corruption of Gawali or Gaoli, a cowherd. The Gaolis, a race either of Hindus or aborigines, were a powerful race at one time in Gondwana, and established a dynasty in the modern Chhindwara district. It is possible that the Gonds learnt something of their civilisation from them, and in some cases—as is suggested by this Epic—found wives among their daughters. Lingo suggests that the four Gonds should go and see fire for themselves. The youngest goes and narrowly escapes a most disagreeable fate. He returns to his brethren, and to Lingo, and tells them what has happened. Lingo himself then determines to go. The description of Lingo playing on his guitar up in a tree (the two-stringed guitar is a favourite instrument with Gonds), while the giant and his wife dance (dancing is a passion with the Gonds and other aborigines of India), is most grotesque and amusing. As a result of his visit he takes away with him the giant's seven daughters to wed with the four Gonds.

He said, "I will show you something; see if anywhere in your waistbands there is a flint; if so, take it out and make fire."

Then they took out pieces of flint and began to make fire,

But the matches did not ignite. As they were doing this, a watch of the night passed.

They threw down the matches, and said to Lingo, "Thou art a saint;

"Show us where our fire is, and why it does not come out."

Lingo said, "Three kōss (six miles) hence is Rikad Gawadi the giant.

"There is fire in his field; where smoke shall appear, go there.

"Come not back without bringing fire." Thus said Lingo.

They said, "We have never seen the place, where shall we go?"

"Ye have never seen where this fire is?" Lingo said;

"I will discharge an arrow thither.

"Go in the direction of the arrow; there you will get fire."

He applied the arrow, and having pulled the bow, he discharged one;

It crashed on, breaking twigs, making its passage clear.

Having cut through the high grass, it made its way and reached the old man's place.

The arrow dropped close to the fire of the old man, who had daughters.

The arrow was near the door. As soon as they saw it, the daughters came and took it up,

And kept it. They asked their father, "When will you give us in marriage?"

Thus said the seven sisters, the daughters of the old man.

"I will marry you as I think best for you;

"Remain as you are"; so said the old man, the Rikad Gawadi.

Lingo said, "Hear, O brethren! I shot an arrow; it made its way.

"Go there, and you will see fire; bring thence the fire."

Each said to the other, "I will not go": but at last the youngest went.

He descried the fire, and went to it; then beheld he an old man looking like the trunk of a tree.

He saw afar the old man's field, around which a hedge was made.

The old man kept only one way to it, and fastened a screen to the entrance, and had a fire in the centre of the field.

He placed logs of the Mahua and Anjan and Saj trees on the fire.

Teak faggots he gathered, and enkindled flame.

The fire blazed up, and, warmed by the heat of it, in deep sleep lay the Rikad Gawadi.

Thus the old man like a giant did appear. When the young Gond beheld him, he shivered;

His heart leaped; and he was much afraid in his mind, and said:

"If the old man were to rise he will see me, and I shall be eaten up;

"I will steal away the fire, and carry it off, then my life will be safe."

He went near the fire secretly, and took a brand of Tembhur wood tree.

When he was lifting it up a spark flew and fell on the hip of the old man.

That spark was as large as a pot: the giant was blistered: he awoke alarmed,

And said, "I am hungry, and I cannot get food to eat anywhere; I feel a desire for flesh;

"Like a tender cucumber hast thou come to me." So said the old man to the Gond,

Who began to fly. The old man followed him. The Gond then threw away the brand which he had stolen.

He ran onward and was not caught. Then the old man, being tired, turned back.

Thence he turned to his field, and came near the fire, sat, and said, "What nonsense is this?

"A tender prey had come within my reach;

"I said, 'I will cut it up as soon as I can,' but it escaped from my hand!

"Let it go! it will come again, then I will catch it. It is gone now."

Then what happened? the Gond returned and came to his brethren,

And said to them, "Hear, O brethren! I went for fire, as you sent me, to that field; I beheld an old man like a giant.

"With hands stretched out and feet lifted up, I ran. I thus survived with difficulty."

The brethren said to Lingo, "We will not go." Lingo said, "Sit ye here.

"O brethren, what sort of a person is this giant. I will go and see him."

So saying, Lingo went away and reached a river.

He thence arose and went onward. As he looked, he saw in front three gourds.

Then he saw a bamboo stick, which he took up.

When the river was flooded,

It washed away a gourd tree, and its seed fell, and each stem produced bottle gourds.

He inserted a bamboo stick in the hollow of the gourd, and made a guitar.

He plucked two hairs from his head, and strung it.

He held a bow, and fixed eleven keys to that one stick, and played on it.

Lingo was much pleased in his mind.

Holding it in his hand, he walked in the direction of the old man's field.

He approached the fire where Rikad Gawadi was sleeping.

The giant seemed like a log lying close to the fire: his teeth were hideously visible;

His mouth was gaping. Lingo looked at the old man, while sleeping.

His eyes were shut. Lingo said, "This is not good time to carry the old man off, while he is asleep."

In front he looked, and turned round and saw a tree

Of the Peepul[1] sort standing erect; he beheld its branches

With wonder, and looked for a fit place to mount upon.

It appeared a very good tree; so he climbed it, and ascended

To the top of it, to sit.

As he sat, the cock crew. Lingo said, "It is daybreak;

"Meanwhile the old man must be rising." Therefore Lingo took the guitar in his hand,

And held it; he gave a stroke, and it sounded well; from it he drew one hundred tunes.

It sounded well, as if he was singing with his voice.

Thus, as it were, a song was heard.

[1] One of the most sacred trees in India.

THE GIANT AND HIS SPOUSE DANCE TO LINGO'S PIPE

Trees and hills were silent at its sound. The music loudly entered into

The old man's ears; he rose in haste, and sat up quickly; lifted up his eyes,

And desired to hear more. He looked hither and thither,

But could not make out whence the sound came.

The old man said, "Whence has a creature come here to-day to sing like the Myna bird?"

He saw a tree, but nothing appeared to him as he looked underneath it.

He did not look up; he looked at the thickets and ravines,

But saw nothing. He came to the road, and near to the fire,

In the midst of the field, and stood.

Sometimes sitting and sometimes standing, jumping and rolling he began to dance.

The music sounded as the day dawned. His old woman came out in the morning, and began to look out.

She heard in the direction of the field a melodious music playing.

When she arrived near the hedge of her field, she heard music in her ears.

The old woman called her husband to her.

With stretched hands and lifted feet, and with his neck bent down, he danced.

Thus he danced. The old woman looked towards her husband, and said, "My old man, my husband,

"Surely that music is very melodious. I will dance," said the old woman.

Having made the fold of her dress loose, she quickly began to dance near the hedge.

Lingo said in his mind, "I am a devout Lingo; God's servant am I.

"I wear my dhotee (cloth round the loins) down to my heels, and keep a knot of hair on my head, and on the navel a diamond, and to my forehead a sacred mark.[1]

"Water may possess a stain, but I have none. I am Lingo. I will make the old man and woman

"To dance the Gond dance. I will sing a song, and cause them to dance, if I be Lingo."

Lingo worshipped his god, and invoked Budhal Pen, Adul Pen,

The sixteen satika (goddesses), and eighteen flags, Manko Rayetal, Jango Rayetal, and Pharsa Pen,[2]

And said, "Salutation to you gods!" He, holding his guitar in his hand, sang various tunes.

"Is my guitar an allurement to them?" So said Lingo. He stopped the guitar.

From on high he saluted the uncle, Rikad Gawadi, the old man;

Who looked towards the top of the tree, and said, "Salutation to you, O nephew.

[1] The knot of hair dedicated to Vishnu and various kinds of sacred marks are commonly seen amongst Hindus.

[2] The names of Gond gods.

"Well hast thou deceived me, and caused us to dance, Whither hast thou come, nephew?"

Lingo going to the old man, held his hand, and said, "Uncle, salutation to you!"

They met together: nephew became known to the uncle, and the uncle to the nephew.

After the meeting was over, the nephew held the uncle's hand.

They both came near the fire and sat. "O nephew, whence hast thou come?" asked the uncle.

"I have killed sixteen scores of deer; we want to roast their liver to eat.

"We were trying to make fire fall from the flint, but fire fell not.

"You possess fire in your field, therefore I discharged an arrow.

"It came near your fire. It arose and fell at the door of your daughters.

"The daughters have lifted it up and carried it away. Have you no sense, uncle?

"I sent my brother to fetch fire, and you ran to eat him.

"If you had caught him you would have eaten him up; and where should I have seen him again?"

The uncle said, "I made a mistake, O nephew, the thing that I did is past."

He replied, "O uncle, I have killed sixteen scores of deer!

Go and eat their flesh as much as you like."

Thus said Lingo. Then the old man said, "Hear, O nephew, my word. There are seven sisters, my daughters;

"I have them here. Take them away, having first bound their eyes."

Lingo then arose, and stood before the uncle and said, "I am going, uncle.

"Receive my salutation." Lingo thence went by the way to the house, where the old man's daughters were.

Having arrived, he stood at the door. Lingo appeared a youth of twelve years.

Or as sixteen years old; in front he looked foppish, like a young man;

From behind he looked like a devout Brahman. He appeared as a good man.

The seven sisters from within the house came to Lingo, and regarded him

As a young man. They came out and stood before Lingo.

"Tell us," said the seven sisters, "who art thou? Tell us."

He said, "Thy father is my uncle, and thy mother is my aunt.

"I am devout Lingo, the servant of God. I am Lingo.

"Here, O sisters! my arrow came to your house and fell; I have been in search of it for a long time.

"My four brothers are sitting in the jungle; and I have killed sixteen scores of deer;

"They are also in the jungle, and my brothers are sitting near them.

"I have come here for fire: it is very late.

"My brothers must be expecting fire; they must have felt hunger,

"And thirsty they must have become; where will they get bread?"

Thus said Lingo. Then the seven sisters, what did they begin to say?

"Hear, O brother, our word. Thou art a son to uncle, and we daughters to aunt.

"There is a good relation between you and us; how can you leave us?

"We will come along with you; therefore, don't say No."

"If you like to come, be ready soon, and take the onward road," said Lingo.

They took the bedding for their beds, and their clothes, and gave the arrow to Lingo,

Lingo in the front, and they in the rear, began to tread the way.

The brothers were sitting and looking, and saying, "When will he come?"

They beheld him from afar; and said, "Hear, O brothers, our Lingo appears!"

They arose and looked, and saw Lingo and behind him the seven sisters.

They said, "With whose daughters, or whose daughters-in-law

"Is he coming? Look, O brethren! they are of good appearance.

"If Lingo give them to us, we would make them our wives." So said the brethren.

Lingo came near and stood, and said, "Hear, O brethren, my word!

"These seven sisters are the daughters of our uncle; they have come;

"Take out your knives, and give to them the liver of the deer."

They took out the livers: some brought faggots and enkindled fire;

On its blaze they roasted flesh, and set it on the ground.

"Offer this liver in the name of God."

So said the four brothers. Lingo arose.

They began to eat, while Lingo did not eat. Then he said,

"Let the seven sisters quickly go back, their father will abuse them.

"Hear, O sisters! Go quickly, or else your mother will abuse you."

They replied, and said, "Hear, O Lingo! Thou who art called good, may we call you bad?

"We will not go, we will stay. Whither thou shalt go, thither we will follow thee."

The brethren said, "Hear, O Lingo, these seven sisters say well!

"Say thou to them, O brother, we will marry them.

"We will make them our wives. Hear, O Lingo, such is our word."

He said, "Take these as wives in marriage, and I shall be greatly pleased.

"Take them here in marriage, I will give you leave to make them your wives."

They said, "If you see any one of them to be good-looking, you take her.

"If any be inferior, we will take her."

He said, "Hear my word, O brothers! I do not need this.

"I promised to give them to you; they are of no use to me."

So said Lingo, "If you marry them they will serve me.

"They will be my sisters-in-law. You are older, and I am younger.

"They can give me water and bread, and spread a bed for me:

"I will sleep on it. They can give me a bath; my clothes they will wash.

"They will be my sisters-in law, and like my mothers they shall be."

So said Lingo. When Lingo said they will be my mothers, the suspicion of the four vanished.

The four Gonds are enamoured with the stalwart daughters of Rikad Gawadi, and desire the saint to tie the marriage knot as speedily as possible. The three elder Gonds are to receive two damsels each, and the youngest, who has but recently escaped from the jaws of his prospective father-in-law, has to be content with one. They return to their village of Kachikopa Lahugad, where the marriage is celebrated according to Gond rites.

They went to Lingo and asked him: "O Lingo, marry us quickly.

"If you marry us, then they are seven sisters, and we are four brothers.

"Distribute to each of us a wife, O Lingo."

He said the three elder should marry two each, and the youngest, only one.

Then said Lingo, "Hear my word, O brethren! In this jungle

"And in this plain how can we make preparation; we have our town, namely, Kachikopa Lahugad:

"We will go there and make preparations for the marriage."

So said Lingo. When they heard this, they departed.

They walked in front, and the women walked behind.

They came to their village Kachikopa Lahugad, and began to make

Preparations. There were no men or women; then Lingo brought water.

He bathed them, boiled turmeric and gave them, and pounded saffron.

He erected a bower, and tied garlands of leaves round it.

He called the four brothers to sprinkle turmeric round about.

He applied turmeric to the four brothers and the seven sisters.

He said, "We cannot marry all at once. Hear, O brothers.

"Let us marry one set only first, and the rest shall work with us for that occasion.

"Then shall the marriage of the second set take place.

"Those who have been already married shall now help us in this marriage ceremony and so on."

This said Lingo; and the four consented to it.

Thus ended the marriage.

The remainder of this portion of the Epic shows how the saintly Lingo, in the absence of the four Gonds who go on a hunting expedition, is subjected to the same temptation which befell the patriarch Joseph in the house of Potiphar. Lingo, like Joseph, rises superior to his temptation, but, unlike Joseph, he administers severe corporal punishment to his temptresses. They in revenge accuse him falsely to their husbands when they return, and the four Gonds in rage slay their benefactor.

"Lingo has done good to us, and brought wives to our houses.

"But Lingo is without a wife, he thought of our good, but not of his own,

"So we will reckon him as our father.

"We will kill game, and bring flowers for Lingo. Let him sit in a swing."

So said the four brothers.

Lingo sat in a swing, and the seven sisters swung the swing.

The four brothers took their bows and arrows and repaired to the jungle.

After that, what happened? The seven sisters said within themselves, "Hear, O sisters. The Lingo

"Is our husbands' younger brother, and we are his sisters-in-law; we are at liberty to laugh with him;

"We can pull him by the hand, and we can make him to speak with us.

"Lingo does not laugh with us; he neither speaks nor looks towards us; he has closed his eyes;

"But he shall laugh, and we will play with him." So saying,

Some held his hand, and some his feet, and pulled him, but Lingo moved not his eyes;

He did not speak or laugh with them.

Then Lingo said to them, "Hear, O sisters. You have held my hands,

"And feet, and pulled them; but remember you are my sisters.

"You are my mothers; why do you deal so with me? I am God's servant.

"I don't care though my life be sacrificed, but I will not

"Speak with you, nor look at you, nor laugh with you." So

Said Lingo. Having heard this

The eldest sister said, "Hear, O sisters. Lingo speaks not to

"Us, looks not towards us."

They began to embrace him. Then Lingo became angry: the anger ascended from the heel to his head.

Thence descended into his eyes and down to his feet. Lingo looked before him,

But saw nothing, save a pestle for cleaning rice.

He descended from his swing and took the pestle in his hand,

And soundly flogged his sisters-in-law. As he was beating them,

The seven sisters began to flee before him, like bellowing cows.

Thence he returned, and having come to his swing,

In a swing he slept. Thus these seven sisters had received a sound beating.

They returned to their house, and having each one gone to her room,

The seven sisters slept in seven places; and Lingo slept in a swing.

Thus noontide came, and the time for the returning of the four brothers arrived.

Some of them had killed an antelope, some a hare, some a peafowl,

Some a quail; some brought flowers.

They came into their house and set their burdens down, and said, "Let us go to our Lingo;

"We will give him flowers; he may be expecting us." They entered the house.

They came near Lingo and stood, and saw him sleeping.

They said, "There is no one here, Lingo is sleeping; our
Wives do not appear.
"Then we will come and awake Lingo." Thence they returned
To their houses, and going to their rooms, they began to
Look.
They, the women, were feigning sleep, and panting as if
Fear had come upon them. Then the husbands asked them,
"Why are you sleeping? and why don't you swing Lingo?" They replied,
"Hear our words
"How Lingo, your brother, dealt with us. How long shall
"We hide this disgrace?
"He allows you to go to the jungle, and behind your back
"He shamefully maltreats us.
"Such is the conduct of this Lingo. We have kept quiet till to-day;
"Now we will not stop quiet. We will go back to our father's
"Place.
"We will not stay here. Can one woman have two husbands?"
The brethren said, "We told Lingo at the first
"That there were seven sisters, and that he might choose one from amongst them,

"And that we would marry the rest. But he said,

"'They are my sisters, they are my mothers.'

"Thus said that sinner, wicked and ill-conducted, that Lingo.

"While we were hunting, he deceived us. We will take

"Him to the jungle, and, having killed him, we will pull out

"His eyes.

"Up to this day we have killed antelope and hares;

"But to-day we go to hunt Lingo, and after killing him we will take out his eyes.

"And we will play with them as with marbles; and then we will eat food and drink water."

Then they came to Lingo, and stood before him and said,

"Rise, O Lingo, our youngest brother!"

Lingo said, "Why brethren—why have you not brought the game and the flowers to me? and why have you come so soon?"

They said, "There is a large animal, we hunted it hard, but it did not fall:

"It does not flee, it stands still only; we are tired of discharging our arrows at it."

Lingo arose from the swing and sat, and looked towards his brothers.

"I will kill that animal." So said Lingo.

Lingo thence arose and came out of the house, and said,

"Come, O brothers. Where is the animal?"

In front, Lingo, and in rear the four brothers walked towards the jungle.

"It is a very large animal," said they; and saying thus, they searched for it among trees and grass.

Lingo went under a Char tree and sat. Then they said

"O brother!

"Sit here, and we will bring water." So saying, yonder they went.

Being amongst the trees they said among themselves, "Good Lingo is seated in the shade,

"This is the right time to effect our desire." The four took four arrows and shot:

One arrow hit the head, and the head split open;

One hit the neck, and it bowed down; one hit the liver, and it was cleft.

Thus Lingo breathed his last!

The four brothers came up to Lingo and stood,

And said, "Draw a knife, and we will take out his eyes."

They drew out a knife and

Took out his eyes, and said, "Cover him."

So they took some twigs and covered Lingo.

Then they said, "We have killed Lingo, who was wicked."

They plucked some green leaves of the tree and made a cup of them,

And placed in it the two eyes of Lingo, and one tied it to his waistband.

They walked towards their house, and at evening time they arrived home.

One said, " Hear, O wives! Kindle fire quickly
" And light a lamp." They drew the stalks of flax from the eaves of the house roof, and enkindled fire.

One said, " It is a fine light, let us play at marbles."

They took out both the eyes, and said, " O seven sisters!

You also join in play."

They brought the eyes, and placed one on the east side and the other on the west;

And the brethren, sitting close, held the marbles between the joints of their fingers,

Then began to play at marbles with the two eyes; and their game lasted an hour.

Part III

THE RESTORATION TO LIFE OF LINGO. AFTER HIS REVIVAL HE DELIVERS THE GOND RACE FROM THEIR IMPRISONMENT

> Ye who love the haunts of Nature
> Love the sunshine of the meadow,
> Love the shadow of the forest,
> Love the wind among the branches,
> And the rain-shower and the snow-storm,
> And the rushing of great rivers.
> Listen to these wild traditions.
>
> —Longfellow.

The third scene of the drama opens in the Upper World. Bhagawan, the great god, who represents Bura Deo, the chief god of the Gond Pantheon, sits in his court and all the minor gods, including two of the Gond gods, Pharsa Pen, and Rayetal his wife, sit near him. They are in a state of consternation. Lingo, beloved of the gods, is dead, and they know not where his body is. The saints, or Rishis, will not, or cannot, assist them to find it. At length Bhagawan, in rage, rouses himself, and having made unpleasant remarks about everyone, performs certain ablutions ; after which he created a wonderful bird, and named it Kagesur, a word apparently of Hindu origin. This bird is sent forth to search everywhere for Lingo. At length he discovers Lingo's body in the neighbourhood of Kachikopa Lahugad. There it lies, smashed by the cruel Gonds, and without eyes. Bhagawan takes nectar, and gives it to the superhuman Gond ancestor Kurtao Sabal,[1] and bids him sprinkle it on the liver, belly, and head of his body. He does so and Lingo revives.

What did god (Bhagawan) do now?

Rayetal, Pharsa Pen, what did they in the upper world?

In the courts of the god all the minor divinities sat.

God spake to them—"Hear, O friends, Can you tell in what world the body of Lingo is fallen?

"Will any of you trace it and go on this errand?"

They made the preparation of betel-nut, and threw it before the saints.

God said, "Take this up, and come and tell me."

But none of the saints took it up.

Then God became angry, and began to reproach them.

God arose, and with a potful of water washed his hands and feet.

After washing, he, from the substance of his body created a crow, and sprinkled water of ambrosia on it,

And thus made it alive, and named it Kagesur; and held it in his hand.

And said, "Go to the jungle and make a search between hills, glen, lanes; amongst trees, in rivers and water."

[1] Another name apparently for Kalia Adao. See page 154.

Thence the crow departed, and roamed over the upper world.

But did not find the body of Lingo anywhere; thence he came to the lower world and began his search.

When it came to the Jungle of Kachikopa Lahugad, it searched in the valleys there.

Its sight fell on the twigs, it came to them and sat, and searched the twigs.

It saw Lingo lying there looking as if smashed, and without eyes.

This the crow observed, and flew away and came to the Upper World.

Perching on God's hand, it sat. God asked it, "Where have you seen him?"

It said, "I came to the jungle of Kachikopa Lahugad, I saw a man there in a cave."

When God heard this he became silent, and understood the truth of it;

And then said, "It was in that very jungle that Lingo was born from a flower of the tree.

And has never been there since." He took nectar

From out of his fingers, and called Kurtao Sabal, and said to him.

"Take this and sprinkle on the liver, belly, and head of the body."

Thus, the crow in front, and Kurtao Sabal behind, went to Kachikopa Lahugad.

Kurtao Sabal said, "Hear, O crow. Here is my Lingo."

KAGESAR SPRINKLES THE BODY OF LINGO

Ambrosia was brought, and dropped into his mouth, and sprinkled over his head and body: then Lingo's head began to unite.

And his flesh became warm.

Lingo rose.

Lingo seems either to have been ignorant as to the cause of his death, or to have been full of the spirit of forgiveness. He asks for his four brothers and learns of their fiendish wickedness. Nothing deterred by this he announces his intention of now going to the rescue of the Gond race, who are imprisoned in Dhawalgiri by Bhagawan.

Lingo sat up. Looking towards the crow, he said, "I was fast asleep.

"Where are my brothers?

"I see only a man and a crow, and I don't see my brothers."

After this

Kurtao Sabal replied, "Where are your brothers?

"You were dead, your body was lying here; we came and restored you to life;

"The brothers you enquire about have killed you, and gone away."

Then said Kurtao Sabal, "What do you say to going?" Lingo addressing the crow, said—

"I will go to my sixteen scores of Gonds.

"I will go and see them, and speak to them."

He starts on his journey. Night overtakes him and he ascends a tree where he remains till daybreak.

The crow and Kurtao Sabal started in one direction.
And Lingo took another road.
Lingo, while crossing the mountains and jungle, was benighted.
Then Lingo said, " I will stay here alone;
" Tigers and bears may devour me."
He went to a large Niroor tree.
When he climbed to the top, the night came on:
Wild cocks crowed, peacocks cried, antelopes were afraid,
And bears wagged their heads, jackals yelled, and the jungle resounded.
At midnight Lingo saw the Moon, and said to himself:
" The day is approaching, and while the Stars are still visible, I will ask them about my Gonds."
At the third watch of the night, the cock crowed:
The morning star appeared, the sky became red.

Lingo descends from his tree at daybreak and asks the Sun where his Gonds are. The Sun cannot tell. He asks the Moon. She, too, is ignorant.

Lingo, descending from the tree, ran towards the Sun and saluted him;

And said, "I want to know where my sixteen scores of Gonds are?"

The Sun said, "I am engaged in the service of God during the four watches of the day,

"And have not seen your Gonds."

Lingo went to the Moon,

Saluted, and asked her if she knew anything

About his sixteen scores of Gonds. The Moon replied:

"I travel all night, and during the day am engaged in the service of God;

"Therefore I know not."

He asks one Kumayat—apparently a Hindu Rishi, who, after speaking most unpleasantly about the Gonds, gives him the information he desires.

Lingo then went to black Kumayat,

Saluted him, and asked him, "Where are my sixteen scores of Gonds,"

He replied: "Hear, Lingo: Mention about anyone but Gonds.

"The Gonds are foolish like the ass,

"They eat cats, mice, and bandicoots;

"They also eat pigs and buffaloes; they are of such a bad caste.

"Why do you ask me about them?

"At the source of the Jumna river, on the Dhawalagiri mountain,
"Mahadeva has caught the Gonds,
"And has confined them in a cave, and shut its mouth with a stone of sixteen cubits long.
"Bhasmasur the giant has been appointed to guard it, and watch the place."

Lingo then underwent a severe penance for twelve months;[1] and having acquired a large amount of merit, proceeds to interview Mahadeva. Much as he desires it, Mahadeva cannot refuse Lingo and at length promises to release them.

After hearing this Lingo set out, and walked night and day,
Making devotion. After twelve months had expired, the term of his devotion was complete,
When the golden seat of Mahadeva began to shake (from the effect of Lingo's devotion).
Then Mahadeva said, "What devotee has come to Dhawalagiri and has performed devotions to me,
"Rendering me under obligation to him?"
As he was wondering and searching,
He went towards Lingo, stood at a distance, and recognised him.
Lingo did not shake his head, or lift his foot, or open his eyes.

[1] The Hindus believe that mortals by severe asceticism can compel the high gods to grant them their requests.

His flesh was consumed; his bones only remained. Thus Lingo was found on the thorns.

Whereupon Mahadeva said,

"What do you ask for?—Ask what you wish, and it will be granted."

Lingo replied:

"I want nothing but my sixteen scores of Gonds."

Mahadeva replied:

"Make no mention of Gonds; but for any kingdom, or for any amount of money which you can enjoy,

"And remember me." Thus said Mahadeva: to which Lingo did not agree.

On his again asking for the Gonds, Mahadeva disappeared, and consented to give them to him,

Saying: "Hear, Lingo. Your Gonds are below the earth, take them away."

Lingo rose, saluted him, and went on. After this,

Narayan said: "Hear, Mahadeva: All these Gonds

"Were well concealed and were forgotten; if they were dead, it would be a pleasure to me.

"If they come out alive from below the earth, they will act as usual:

"They will eat buffaloes, birds, such as pigeons, crows, and eagles, and vultures.

"They will alight here and there; smells will arise, bones will be scattered, and make the earth look very bad.

"The respect for mount Dhawalagiri will be lost."

Mahadeva, hearing this, replied: "Hear, Narayan, I have passed my word.

"I have erred, but will not change my word."

Narayan the high god hears of Mahadeva's promise and is much upset by it. He pictures the dirt and disorder which will arise in Dhawalagiri once the Gonds are released.

He will only consent to the Gond's release if Lingo brings him as an offering the young of the black-bird Bindo for an offering. This magical bird lived by the sea-shore. It and its mate lived luxuriously on the brains of elephants, camels and other animals. Its deadly foe was a sea-serpent called Bhournag, which had repeatedly rifled its nest, and destroyed seven broods of its young. This fable, it is believed, is of Hindu origin, and some think it refers to the bird Garuda of Hindu mythology, which was a remorseless enemy of the serpent race.

Narayan then addressed Lingo—

"Hear, Lingo. Bring me the young ones of the black-bird Bindo for an offering;

"After that you may take the Gonds away."

Lingo went and reached the sea, where there was nothing but water visible;

And on the shore he saw the young ones of the black-bird.

The parent bird

Had gone to the jungle. This bird was such, that
For food it killed the elephant, and ate its eyes; and
Breaking its head, brought the brains for the young ones to eat.
There had been seven broods, at seven different times;
But they had been devoured by a sea-serpent, called the
Bhournag. Lingo went near.

Lingo goes and slays the mighty snake. The parents return and, not knowing what Lingo has done, are about to kill him, as he sleeps. The young birds tell them of his powers, and in gratitude they agree to take their young to Mahadeva.

After seeing the young ones, he said to himself: "If I take them in the
"Absence of their parents, I shall be called a thief; I will therefore
"Take them in the presence of the parents, and will be true to my name."
He slept near the young birds with comfort.
A large snake, as thick as the trunk of the Itumna tree appeared,
With a hood as large as a basket for winnowing corn. This serpent, called the Bhournag, came out of the water to eat the young ones.
The young ones were terrified on seeing the serpent, and began to cry.

Lingo, taking an arrow, and fixing it in his bow,
Shot the serpent, and then cut it into seven pieces, which he immediately
Brought and laid at the head of his bed, and covered them up.
Then the male and female of the black-bird returned from the jungle.
They brought the carcass of some camels and some elephants, together with some eyes and lips of elephants,
As food for their young ones.
But the young ones refused to eat;
When the female said to the male:
"Notwithstanding my having had seven times,
"I am like a barren she-buffalo; if these young ones are spared
"I shall be like a mother of children. What evil eye has been cast on
"My young ones, that they do not eat!"
The male bird, alighting from the tree, saw a white object lying below, where was Lingo.
He then exclaimed: "Here is a man, and that is why our young ones do not eat.
"Let us kill him and extract his brains;
"Our young ones will then take their food."
Hearing this, the young ones said:
"You have brought food for us, but how shall we eat it? You are our parents,
"You leave us alone, and go away to the jungle;
"Who is there to protect us?

"The serpent came to eat us.

"This man whom you see, has saved our lives.

"Give him first to eat, we will then take our food; unless he eats, we will not eat."

After hearing what the young ones said,

The mother flew down from the tree, and coming near Lingo,

And lifting up the cloth with which he had covered himself saw the seven pieces of the Bhournag serpent.

Seeing this she began to exclaim:

"This is the serpent that has always eaten my young ones, and rendered me childless!

"Had this man not been here it would have devoured these also."

Addressing Lingo, she said: "Rise, father—rise, brother; who are you, and

"Where have you come from? You have saved the lives of our young ones, and you have become our grandfather.

"Whatever you say, we will listen to it."

He said:

"O bird, I am a devotee, a worshipper of the Deity."

"Tell us," the bird said, "what has brought you here."

Lingo replied, "I want your young ones."

On hearing this the bird began to cry bitterly,

And, opening her eyes, she said:

"I would give you anything

"Except my young ones."

Lingo said:
"I will take your young ones merely to show them to Mahadeva."
In reply to this, the black Bindo said:
"If Mahadeva wants us, I am ready to go."

Lingo has a delightful journey on this mythical aeroplane back to Mahadeva. The female bird takes her young birds on one wing and Lingo on the other. The male bird flies above them and protects from the sun.

Saying this, the female bird carried the young ones on one wing,
And Lingo on the other. The male Bindo then said, "Hear, me, Lingo;
"You will feel the effects of the sun, why then should I remain here?"
The female Bindo then flew towards the sea,
The male Bindo flying over her, and using his wings as a shelter for Lingo.
It was six months' journey to the residence of Mahadeva; but starting in the morning
They alighted at midday in the court-yard of Mahadeva.
Narayan, seeing them from the door, went to Mahadeva and said:
"Here is Lingo and the black Bindo birds which he has brought."
Mahadeva then released the Gonds.
Mahadeva exclaimed: "O Narayan!

LINGO'S WONDERFUL FLIGHT

"I foresaw this, and you would not believe me when I told you

"That Lingo would bring the bird."

Mahadeva then said: "Hear, Lingo: I give you back your sixteen scores of Gonds;

"Take them, and go away."

Lingo then saluted Mahadeva and went to the cave, and taking the name of the great god,

And that of the god Rayetal, he made Bhasmasur, the giant, to walk in front of him.

Reaching the cave, he lifted up the stone, sixteen cubits long, and laid it aside.

The Gonds coming out of the cave and seeing Lingo, cried,

"We have no one but you."

Mahadeva gave flour of wheat to some, flour of millet to others,

And rice to others.

The Gonds went to the river, and began preparing their food.

Some of the Gonds said that they had been confined and punished severely.

On hearing this, Lingo said:

"You are now at the river, cook and eat, and then complain."

Part IV

LINGO SUBDIVIDES THE GONDS INTO TRIBES: AND INSTITUTES THE WORSHIP OF THEIR GODS.

LINGO PASSES

Soon my task will be completed,
Soon your footsteps I shall follow,
To the Islands of the Blessed,
To the Kingdom of Ponemah,
To the Land of the Hereafter.
—LONGFELLOW.

THE Gonds, after their liberation, set out with Lingo from Dhawalagiri, near the source of the Jumna, for Kachikopa Lahugad, in the Satpuras. They came to a river whose flood was increasing rapidly. All save Lingo and the four Gonds got across safely. These were still far from safety when Dame, the tortoise, and Pusi the alligator, invited them to sit on their backs, and promised to convey them across in safety. They accepted the invitation and the four Gonds sat on the alligator's back, while Lingo mounted the tortoise. In mid-stream Pusi the alligator, treacherously tried to drown the four Gonds in anticipation of a substantial meal. They cried to Lingo, who went to their assistance. They were saved and, along with Lingo, cross the stream on the tortoise's back. The tortoise, it must be noted, is a sacred animal or "totem" to the Gonds. No religious Gond would hunt, kill, or eat the tortoise.

Lingo kneaded the flour and made it into a thick cake, and cooked pulse, and satisfied all the Gonds.

Then clouds arose, and it began to rain.

When the rivers flooded, and the flood began to roll, all the Gonds spoke:

"O Lingo, much rain has come up and is falling."

Then all these Gonds began to walk in the middle of the river;

From among all these Gonds, four persons with Lingo remained.

Lingo, having seen this, began to say: "Hear, O brethren;

"This river is flooded, how shall we cross it?"

More clouds came up, and darkness fell;

Then those four persons and Lingo began to speak:

"Hear, O brethren, what shall we do, and how shall we go on? The day is departing."

Now Dame the Tortoise, and Pusi the Alligator, were playing in the water.

They came to them out of the water, and began to speak;

"Hear, O brethren, why do you silently stand and cry?"

They said: "Our sixteen scores of Gonds have all gone and we only have remained;

"O brethren, how shall we go?" They said:

"Sit on us, and we will take you across.

"If you keep your oath we will take you across the river."

They replied: "Hear, O sisters. You are Pusi the Alligator, and you Dame the Tortoise.

"Those four persons who are before you will keep their oath first of all.

"If any beat you we will not allow it, if any try to catch you we will prevent it.

"You shall be the eldest sister of us four persons," said they.

Dame the Tortoise, and Pusi the Alligator, came up to them, and the four Gonds sat on the Alligator's back, leaving Lingo alone to sit on the back of the Tortoise.

The Alligator went first, and then followed the Tortoise in the flood.

The wicked Alligator, having taken them into the midst of the water, began to drown them.

They began to cry. Then the Tortoise spoke: "Hear, O Lingo,

"Stretch thy hand and drag them off, and make them sit on my back."

Lingo, having stretched his hand, caught them and dragged them away, and made them sit on the Tortoise's back.

Then the Tortoise took the four men on his back and went across the river;

And they fell at its feet, and said: "Hear, O Tortoise, we will not become faithless to you."

The Gonds then began, under Lingo's instruction, to settle down to a civilised life. They built

LINGO AND THE FOUR GONDS CROSS THE RIVER

houses, prepared fields, held bazaars, and adopted an agricultural life.

Then those four went by a jungly path, and ascended one hill,
And descended another. Thus they went forward.
They began to cut trees and build houses, and they remained not together, but here and there.
Fields and houses were formed by the Gonds, and their town became large.
A bazaar (periodical market) was held in Nar Bhumi (the name of the town).
Then Lingo began to say: "Hear, O brethren. If you will sow millet, it will spring up."
Thus twelve months passed, and Nar Bhumi began to appear excellent.
Those who had no bullocks received them.
Those who had no carts received carts: thus all the houses of the city became prosperous.

Then Lingo called them together, and upbraiding them for their ignorance of ordinary relationships, divided them into families or tribes, in part doubtless for marriage purposes. The actual classification of tribes adopted by the Gonds was, according to Hislop, into twelve classes. The classification in the Epic corresponds only partially with this. To one tribe Lingo gives the name of Manakwaja, which means one who fashions "images of gods." To another tribe he gives the name of Dahukwaja, which means "drum-soldiers or musicians." Other names which Lingo gives, Koilabutal, Koikopal, Kolami, Kotolyal, are names still given to Gond tribes, Koorkus and Bhils, though aborigines of Dravidian origin, are now considered quite distinct from Gonds. Koorkus, however, still live in the Satpuras, and Bhils are found in the most western portions of the hilly country.

All the Gonds came to Lingo, and sat close to each other in rows.

While Lingo stood in the midst of them, and began to speak:

"Hear, O brethren. All you Gonds understand nothing.

"You do not know whom to call brother, and whom father,

"Or other relative; from whom to ask a daughter, and to whom to give your daughter;

"With whom to laugh." Then those Gonds began to say:

"O Lingo, you possess great and good understanding; do as you

"Have said with all your might, and make tribes of us."

Then Lingo, out of the sixteen scores of the Gonds, separated four score, and told them to rise.

He caught one of them by the hand, and said:

"O friend, become Manakwaja."

Then that man became Manakwaja. Then he caught another by the hand, and said: "Become, O friend, Dahukwaja":

And he became Dahukwaja. He then caught

Another by the hand, and said: "O friend, be Koilabutal," and he became Koilabutal.

Then he caught another by the hand, and said: "You become a wild Koikopal";

And he became Koikopal. Thus the four scores were divided.

Out of the remaining twelve bands, four more were separated.

The first band he made to be Koorkus, and the others he made to be Bhils.

The third he made to be Kolami, and the fourth he made to be Kotolyal. Thus eight bands

Were divided.

Then follows a rather obscure passage in which Lingo instructs the Gonds in their worship. It was the Hindu month of Weishak (May). A goat of five years old, a crowing cock, a three-year old calf, and a cow two years old, are brought together for the sacrifice. The sacrifice of the calf and cow are, it must be remembered, abhorrent to the Hindus, but were apparently common amongst the Gonds of early days. Two bards, or minstrels, "Manozas," are summoned. The idol god, "Ghahara Pen" (or the bell god), is one of the Gond gods. His idol is formed by stringing together a set of small tinkling bells. The Sacred Fan, wherewith to fan the gods, is also brought. The next idol god to be made is Parsapot, a name for Pharsa Pen. His image is made of iron—commonly found in the Satpuras. He is represented by a spear, and is still worshipped by Gonds. The next idol god is the Stick god, made of the bamboo.

Arrived, then Lingo said: "Come, O brethren, we cannot see God

"Anywhere; let us make a god, and we will worship him."

Then all the Gonds with one voice

Said: "Yes, O brethren, bring a goat

"Five years old, a crowing cock one year old, a three-year old calf, a cow

"Two years old; and call two of the

"Manozas (bards)." Then they named one god Ghahara Pen (the Bell god).

Lingo said: "Bring a chouri (fan) made from the tail of the wild cow."

"Then," said Lingo, "open the shop of the ironsmith, and make the god Parsapot of steel.

"Go to the jungle and cut a bamboo stick, and bring it."

Lingo then bathed in a dhotee, and applied the sacred tika, or mark, to his forehead, both of which rites are clearly borrowed from Hinduism. Lingo then called two of the Drummer tribe to the assistance of the minstrels. A strange piece of ritual is enacted. The Chain god, an idol made of an iron chain, and worshipped by Gonds as Sakla Pen, is then bound to one Stick god, and Pharsa Pen, the Iron god, is bound to another Stick god. Then the Sacred Fan is waved over it, and Pharsa Pen is worshipped. Two other female members of the Gond Pantheon, Manko Rayetal and Jango Rayetal, probably wives of Pharsa Pen, appear. Lingo behaves like one possessed; a sight commonly seen amongst Gond devotees.

In the morning Lingo arose and went to a river, and bathed, and wore a dhotee (a cloth round the loins),

And applied the tika (sacred mark) to his forehead.

"What!" says he. "Hearken, O brethren, to the Ozas (bards).

"Call two Dahaking drummers"; and they called them, and brought the Stick god. Then

Lingo bound the Chain god to the stick, and placed another

Stick in the god Pharsapot; and the Gungawan Chouri (the Cow-tailed fan) was waved over it; and with joined hands

They said: "Hail! Pharsa Pen."

He lifted the stick, and the goddesses Manko Rayetal, Jango Rayetal,

And Pharsa Pen came, and stood there; and Lingo was possessed of them.

Then Lingo became a man devoted to god, and moved and jumped much:

Lingo was in front, and behind were goats, cocks, a calf.
And all the Gonds
Assembled in one place.

Then leaving the village of Dhanegaon, they went, in rude procession, into the forest with their gods, the sacred string of bells, the sacred spear, the sacred chain, the sacred fan. The Stick god leads the way. Then the bearers of these consecrated emblems are ordered to stop. The sacrificial ceremonies here described are still practised by the Gonds.

They came, and began to say, "This is a thick jungle."
Then the Gonds called on the gods to stand still.
They fell at the feet of the gods, and asked where they
Should make seats for the gods of each band.
Then all the Gonds came in front and, with joined hands,
Stood;
And began to ask Pharsa Pen; who replied: "Hear, O brethren,
"Between twelve glens and seven dales[1] go, and make place for us gods."
Then in front went the Stick god, and behind followed all the Gonds.

[1] The Satpuras mean seven valleys or dales.

They arrived, and after alighting they began to pick up grass and lift stones.

Then said Lingo,

"Hear, O brethren, Do you see yonder a

Bijesal tree? Go and cut it and make a kettle-drum from its wood." They, taking an axe, went and cut it.

Some held a pitcher, and brought a pitcherful of water;

Some digged earth, and

Made a platform, and placed on it the Stick god. Some said

"Our drum is not ready.

"Burn this fire in front, and light the lamp."

They wetted five tolas' weight of vermilion in ghee, and

Threw five tolas of rāl (resin) on the fire.

Then sat Lingo with joined hands before the god Ghahara,

The Bell god.

Ghahara Pen began to jump about, and possessed the body of Lingo. Pharsa Pen began to play also.

Then they took a pitcherful of daru (liquor),

And sprinkled it on the stick, and said: "Hail to you, Pharsa Pen!"

And, with joined hands, they fell at his feet. While they

Were falling at his feet,

The goddess Rayetal possessed the body of Lingo, who moved

And danced much.

Then he began to speak thus: "Bring to me victims—

"Goats of five years old." After bringing the goat they

Fell at his feet.

And washed its head, and applied vermilion, and poured

Daru (liquor), into its ears.

Then after catching the goat by the feet, they threw it

Before the god.

And the goddess Rayetal possessed the body of the goat,

Which began to shake its head, ears, and whole frame very much.

Then two or four persons ran and caught it, and threw it

Down,

Before the goddess, and killed it. Then blood was sprinkled

Around.

And they placed the head before the goddess, and took the

Body.

Then a white cock, a year old, was brought, and they killed

It.

And began to play a good tune on the Kingree (a one-stringed guitar), and the drum.

The goddess derived pleasure therefrom. Then two feet of

A calf were washed, and so was its mouth; vermilion was
Applied to its forehead.
Then they threw the other animal down, and killed them too.
The head of the calf was placed before the goddess. Then
Said Lingo: "Hear, O brethren;
Remove quickly the skin of the calf, and roast its liver."
They brought stones and made an oven, and placed a pitcher
On it.
The pitcher was filled with water, and flesh was put in it.
The leaves of a tree were cut and brought, and made into plates.
And in a brass-plate they placed cooked rice, liver, flesh,
And they lighted four lamps, and took and placed them
Before the gods.
Some made an offering of silver up to the knee pieces as
A present to the god.
Thus a heap of silver up to the knee of a man was
Gathered before the god.

Then follows a passage in glorification of the Pardhans, or priest caste, introduced by the

Pardhan reciter of the song. The present of a horse is a mark of high honour. The Horse god, Kodan Pen, is sometimes worshipped by the Gonds, and sacred images of the animal are to be seen in the Chanda district. The Pardhans are notorious for their averseness to any kind of labour.

Then Lingo spoke: "Hear, O brethren: The offerings are
"Good in the courts of the god.
"There is no one to receive these offerings.
" Hear, O brethren: From the midst of all these Gonds some
"One should become a Pardhan.
"And we will give this offering to him."
Then Lingo looked well among the company and saw an old,
Hoary-haired man, first of all;
And having looked on him, held his hand and said:
"Become a Pardhan, and we will give you much wealth and
"Clothes;
"We will give you a horse, and whatever you ask us we will
"Not refuse."
"Well, brother," said the old man, "I am fit for nothing
"But to sit and eat."

All saluted him; and some gave clothes, some gave silver pieces,
Some gave him a pipe.

Lingo then divided the Gond tribes into families of seven, six, five, and four. This division, which at first sight seems obscure, refers to the groups or families among the Gonds, which consist of people who worship seven gods, six gods, five gods, or four gods. These sects, or septs, influence their marriage arrangements, as a seven-god worshipper cannot marry one of the class of seven-god worshippers, but must select a partner from one of the other classes.

As they were rising Lingo said: "Hear, O brethren and friends."
Then said they, "What shall we do, O brethren?" He rose and made
Seven persons out of them to stand aside, and said to them:
"You become a family of seven."
He then made six persons to stand aside,
And said, "You become a family of six." He took five more aside,
And made them to stand, and breaking surface of the earth, a family of five were formed.
To the remaining four he said: "Be divided into families of four and five."

Then Lingo, having accomplished his task, and having solemnly bade the Gonds to keep faith with their " totem " the tortoise, departed to the gods.

It is to be feared that Lingo's last admonition about the treatment of the tortoise has been forgotten, for many Gonds in the present day show no respect for the tortoise, eating it as readily as they do other animals.

After saying this, he reminded them to keep
their promise with the Tortoise.
Then they all made salutation. Lingo said:
" O brethren, look yonder towards the gods."
All persons looked behind, but Lingo vanished
and went to the gods.
While they were looking behind, they said
" Where is our Lingo gone ? "

There is much to charm one in this old-world story. Its sympathy with the jungle, its appreciation of the beauty of nature, and the quiet humour of those who take part in its little dramas, all serve to make it peculiarly attractive. Those who know the Gonds, and, indeed, most Indian aborigines, well know their child-like sense of humour, and love of a joke, and how in this respect they differ from the sadder, if wiser, Hindus.

There is a deeper side also to the story of Lingo, which no one interested in " things of the soul " can fail to appreciate. The story invites the Gonds to think that they owed their simple civilisation to a being of a higher order than

THE SACRED POOL AT AMARKANTAK

themselves. Archbishop Whately was wont to say that, without some kind of revelation, the savage could not have risen from his low condition. The story, too, claims for the "emancipator" a wonderfully noble character. "Lingo was a perfect man, water may be stained, but no stain had Lingo." His rejection of temptation—in this respect the story is strangely like that of the patriarch Joseph,—his freedom from malice and guile, his readiness to forgive his murderers, to forget their ingratitude and injuries, and to complete his mission of the rescue of the Gond race, remind one strangely of Him who came not to be ministered unto, but to minister, and to give His Life a ransom for many.

Whether the story came from the soul of some forgotten bard, a soul naturally Christian; whether it contains within it faint echoes of Christian teaching, which had crept into India by unsuspected ways in days gone by, we cannot say. All that we need say is that the story is but one of many proofs that even amongst earth's simplest children noble and true and inspired ideas have some recognition, and that, when the time comes for the fuller enlightenment of such simple people, the Christian teacher will have a soil not wholly barren and unprepared on which to build his lofty spiritual and ethical teaching.